DIRECT HITS

Core Vocabulary of the SAT

VOLUME 1

Fifth Edition

For more information, please contact us by mail:

Direct Hits Publishing
2639 Arden Rd., Atlanta GA 30327

Ted@DirectHitsPublishing.com

Or visit our website:
www.DirectHitsPublishing.com

Fifth Edition: September 2012

ISBN: 978-1-936551-13-2

Edited by Ted Griffith
Cover Design by Carlo da Silva
Interior Design by Alison Rayner

ACKNOWLEDGEMENTS

This fifth edition reflects the collaborative efforts of an outstanding team of students, educators, reviewers, and project managers, each committed to helping young people attain their highest aspirations. Their insights and talents have been incorporated into this latest version of *Direct Hits*.

We wish to express our gratitude to Melissa Irby and Mary Catherine Lindsay, who researched, refined, and updated many of the examples used in the books.

We are grateful to educator Susan Maziar for her valuable insights, gleaned from her tutoring experience and from taking the SAT and ACT, and to Jane Armstrong for her editing and eloquent wordsmithing. We also thank Dr. Gavin Drummond for his extensive literary knowledge in updating and enhancing the examples in the book.

Alison Rayner was responsible for creating our interior design. We thank her not only for her creative talent, but also for her flexibility through multiple revisions. Additionally, we are grateful to Carlo da Silva, who once again used his artistic and graphic skills to design our distinctive cover.

Jane Saral's extensive experience as an English teacher and writing instructor enhanced our literary content and expertly guided our editing and proof-reading efforts. We thank her for her diligence and patience throughout this process. We will never look at the Oxford Comma the same way again!

A big thank you goes out to Luther Griffith for his oversight, ensuring that schedules were adhered to and deadlines were met.

Finally, an extra-special thank you to Claire Griffith for her extraordinary work in coordinating and directing the team, compiling the material for the revisions, her creative ideas, and her constant focus on the highest quality content. Without her, this book would not have been possible.

Ted Griffith, Editor

TABLE OF CONTENTS

INTRODUCTION

Why is vocabulary important, you ask?

Words are our tools for learning and communicating. A rich and varied vocabulary enables us to…

Speak more eloquently…

Describe more vividly…

Argue more compellingly…

Articulate more precisely…

Write more convincingly.

Research has proven that a powerful and vibrant vocabulary has a high correlation with success in school, business, the professions, and standardized tests including the PSAT, SAT, SSAT, and AP exams. Yet many students complain that taking the PSAT or SAT is like trying to understand a foreign language. They dread memorizing long lists of seemingly random words.

Their frustration is understandable.

Direct Hits Core Vocabulary of the SAT offers a different approach. Each word is illustrated through relevant examples from popular movies, television, literature, music, historical events, and current headlines.

Students can place the words in a context they can easily understand and remember.

Building on the success of previous editions, the authors of *Direct Hits Core Vocabulary of the SAT* have consulted secondary school teachers, tutors, parents, and students from around the world to ensure that these words and illustrations are exactly on target to prepare you for success on the SAT. You will find that the approach is accessible, effective, and even fun!

Direct Hits offers **selective** vocabulary using **relevant** examples with **vivid** presentation so you can achieve successful **results** on standardized tests and in life.

Let's get started!

CHAPTER 1

Core Vocabulary I   *1 – 50*

The English language contains just over one million words—the most of any language in human history. If each of these words had an equal chance of being used on the SAT, studying for the test would be a truly impossible task.

Fortunately, the pool of words used by Educational Testing Service (ETS) test writers is actually relatively small. Questions on the test are ranked by level of difficulty from 1 to 5, with 5 being the most difficult. In general, level 3 and 4 questions are missed by over half of the test-takers.

These crucial mid-level words, the level 3 and 4 words, form the core **LEXICON** or special vocabulary you need to know to score well on the Critical Reading portion of the SAT. After a careful analysis of recent tests, we have identified 100 Core Vocabulary Words. The first 50 of these words are in Chapter 1, and the second 50 are in Chapter 2. The division is arbitrary. Each word is a high-frequency word that you absolutely must know.

1 | AMBIVALENT
Having mixed or opposing feelings at the same time

In *The Avengers*, Tony Stark, Steve Rogers, Bruce Banner, and Thor are initially **AMBIVALENT** about joining S.H.I.E.L.D.'s Avenger Initiative. While they know it is necessary to recover the Tesseract from Loki, they fear that their contrasting personalities will be detrimental to the group's success. Thor's **AMBIVALENCE** about working with the Avengers comes from the fact that he is **CONFLICTED** (uncertain, torn) about fighting his brother Loki.

In the movie *The Notebook*, Allie has to choose between Noah and Lon. She is emotionally torn by her **AMBIVALENT** feelings as she tells Noah, "There is no easy way; no matter what I do, somebody gets hurt." She later reiterates her **AMBIVALENT** feelings when she tells Lon, "When I'm with Noah, I feel like one person, and when I'm with you, I feel like someone totally different."

KNOW YOUR ROOTS		
LATIN PREFIX: **AMBI** | **both**	AMBIDEXTROUS	able to use both hands with equal ease, skillful, versatile
	AMBIGUOUS (Word 21)	having two or more possible meanings, doubtful, dubious, EQUIVOCAL (Word 210)
	AMBIVALENT	being simultaneously of two minds

2 | ANOMALY
Deviation from the norm or what is expected

ANOMALOUS
ATYPICAL, full of ANOMALIES

The Big Bang Theory is a television show that follows the trials and tribulations of an **ATYPICAL** group of friends in Pasadena, California. The group consists of Leonard, an experimental physicist; Sheldon, a theoretical physicist; Howard, an aerospace engineer; Raj, a particle astrophysicist; and Penny, a waitress at The Cheesecake Factory. Can you guess who the **ANOMALY** is? Penny's presence in the group is **ANOMALOUS** for many reasons; besides being a girl, she is trendy and popular and a little **NAÏVE** (Word 44), whereas the men are geeky, **RECLUSIVE** (Word 113), and VERY **ASTUTE** (perceptive, shrewd). It's humorous to see these **DIVERSE** (of various kinds) friends spend time together because of their continual disagreements.

3 | SARCASTIC, SARDONIC, SNIDE
Mocking; derisive; taunting; stinging

Winston Churchill was famous for his **SARCASTIC** and **SARDONIC** comments. Here are two well-known examples:

Bessie Braddock: Sir, you are a drunk.

Churchill: Madame, you are ugly. In the morning I shall be sober, and you will still be ugly.

Nancy Astor: Sir, if you were my husband, I would give you poison.

Churchill: If I were your husband, I would take it.

In the movie *Avatar*, Dr. Grace Augustine tells Jake, "Just relax and let your mind go blank. That shouldn't be too hard for you." This **SNIDE** remark reveals Grace's initial contempt for Jake.

4 | DEARTH, PAUCITY
A scarcity or shortage of something

Critics and moviegoers alike have observed that there is an overall **DEARTH** of respect for animated features in the Academy Awards. Despite the recent technological and artistic advances in animation, only three animated films have ever been nominated for the **COVETED** (Word 32) Best Picture title: *Beauty and the Beast*, *Up*, and *Toy Story 3*. None of them won the award. Critics were shocked that the phenomenal Pixar film *WALL-E* was not nominated for Best Picture. Though the Academy honors animation through the Best Animated Feature award, industry members speculate that the Best Animated Feature category will perpetuate the **PAUCITY** of animated films nominated for the Best Picture award.

5 | PRATTLE

To speak in a foolish manner; to babble incessantly

Tip for a Direct Hit

The word "rattle" is hidden inside of PRATTLE. If you remember the baby toy, it can help you to remember how babies PRATTLE when they are young: "goo goo, gaa gaa."

Michael Scott of *The Office* served as the regional manager of the Scranton branch of Dunder Mifflin Paper Company. He was most notable, however, for his **INCOHERENT** (Word 185) rambling and often inappropriate remarks. Here is an example of Michael Scott's **PRATTLING** as he discusses his relationship with his employees:

"*My philosophy is basically this. And this is something that I live by. And I always have. And I always will. Don't ever, for any reason, do anything to anyone, for any reason, ever, no matter what. No matter ... where. Or who, or who you are with, or where you are going, or ... or where you've been ... ever. For any reason, whatsoever.*"

6 | WRY, DROLL

Dry; humorous with a clever twist and a touch of irony

Tip for a Direct Hit

A WRY sense of humor is different from a JOCULAR sense of humor. A WRY joke appeals to your intellect and often produces a knowing smile. In contrast, a JOCULAR joke appeals to your funny bone and produces a belly laugh.

George Bernard Shaw once sent Winston Churchill some tickets for the first night of one of his plays. Churchill then sent Shaw a **WRY** response, "Cannot come first night. Will come second night if you have one."

Shaw's response was equally **WRY**: "Here are two tickets for the second night. Bring a friend if you have one."

Even though he did not win, Top Chef contestant Hugh Acheson's **DROLL** one-liners have helped him to become a guest judge on the new TV show *Just Desserts*. He says "I've got youth and **PANACHE** (Word 81) and one eyebrow on my side," referring to his famous trademark unibrow.

7 | UNCONVENTIONAL, UNORTHODOX
Not ordinary or typical; characterized by avoiding customary conventions and behaviors

Katy Perry, Lady Gaga, and Nicki Minaj are known for their catchy hits and bold, **UNCONVENTIONAL** wardrobes. The concert film *Katy Perry: Part of Me*, displayed some of Katy's colorful, **UNORTHODOX** costumes, including a dress covered in spinning peppermints, an ice cream cone hat, and a peacock dress.

Lady Gaga is also known for wearing **UNCONVENTIONAL** and even **OUTLANDISH** (bizarre, outrageous) stage outfits. Some of her most famous **UNORTHODOX** outfits include a coat made of Kermit the Frog dolls and a dress made entirely out of meat.

Some of rapper Nicki Minaj's recent **UNCONVENTIONAL** outfits include a gumball machine-inspired dress and a dress covered in pom-poms. Nicki frequently sports a towering beehive hairstyle, an **HOMAGE** (tribute) to Marge Simpson's famous blue beehive.

8 | METICULOUS, PAINSTAKING, FASTIDIOUS
Extremely careful; very EXACTING

The Wizarding World of Harry Potter at Universal Studios in Florida is a **METICULOUS** recreation of Hogwarts castle and nearby Hogsmeade village. The park's designers spared no expense to **PAINSTAKINGLY** recreate such iconic rooms as Dumbledore's office and the Defense Against the Dark Arts classroom. **ENTHRALLED** (fascinated) visitors can sample butterbeer and even purchase a wand at Ollivander's Wand Shop.

A **FASTIDIOUS** person takes **METICULOUS** to the next level by being overparticular and **EXACTING**. Many car owners are **FASTIDIOUS** about keeping their cars spotless.

9 | AUDACIOUS
Fearlessly, often recklessly daring; very bold

What do American General George Washington and Japanese Admiral Isoroku Yamamoto have in common? Both launched **AUDACIOUS** surprise attacks on unsuspecting adversaries. On Christmas Day 1776, Washington ordered the Colonial Army to cross the Delaware and attack the British and Hessian forces at Trenton. Washington's **AUDACIOUS** plan shocked the British and restored American morale.

On December 7, 1941, Yamamoto ordered the Japanese First Air Fleet to launch a surprise attack on the American Pacific Fleet based at Pearl Harbor. Although Japan's **AUDACIOUS** sneak attack temporarily **HOBBLED** (hampered) the U.S. fleet, it aroused the now-unified country to demand revenge.

10 | INDIFFERENT, APATHETIC
Marked by a lack of interest or concern; NONCHALANT (Word 74)

In the movie *Ferris Bueller's Day Off*, the economics teacher Ben Stein delivers a **SOPORIFIC** (sleep-inducing) lecture on tariffs and the Great Depression. Stein's bored and **INDIFFERENT** students ignore his monotone lecture. Hoping for some sign of interest, Stein tries asking questions, but his efforts are **FUTILE** (Word 46). Some students are so **APATHETIC** they fall asleep.

In *The Great Gatsby*, Tom Buchanan and his wife, Daisy, appear utterly **INDIFFERENT** to each other; indeed, until Tom's ego is challenged by Jay Gatsby's interest in his wife, Tom and Daisy seem **APATHETIC** about improving their damaged marriage.

11 | DIFFIDENT, SELF-EFFACING
Hesitant due to a lack of self-confidence; unassertive; shy; retiring

Many actors and actors confess to being **DIFFIDENT** in their private lives, despite the fact that they make their livings performing in front of audiences, often in **FLAMBOYANT** (Word 81) ways. **SELF-EFFACING** is not what most people think of when they watch Lady Gaga, but apparently even Gaga wakes up feeling insecure and **DIFFIDENT**.

But she then tells herself, "You're Lady Gaga; you get up and walk the walk today."

As you study for the SAT, don't hang back shyly. Don't **SUCCUMB** (give in) to insecurity. Study your *Direct Hits* vocabulary and approach the test with **APLOMB** (Word 318).

12 | PRAGMATIC
Practical; sensible; NOT idealistic or romantic

What do the 16th century French king Henry IV and the 20th century American president Franklin Delano Roosevelt have in common? Both leaders made **PRAGMATIC** decisions that helped resolve a crisis. Henry IV was the newly-crowned Protestant king in a country dominated by Catholics. For the sake of his war-weary country, Henry IV **PRAGMATICALLY** chose to become a Catholic, saying, "Paris is worth a Mass."

In 1933, FDR was a newly-elected president in a country facing the worst economic crisis in its history. For the sake of his country, Roosevelt **PRAGMATICALLY** chose to replace traditional laissez-faire economic policies with "bold, persistent experimentation." FDR **PRAGMATICALLY** explained, "It is common sense to take a method and try it; if it fails, admit it frankly and try another. But above all, try something."

13 | EVOCATION
An imaginative re-creation of something; a calling forth

What do the treasures of Pharaoh Tutankhamen, Taylor Swift's music video "Love Story," and the movie *Titanic* all have in common? They are all powerful **EVOCATIONS**. The treasures of Pharaoh Tutankhamen **EVOKE** the power and splendor of Ancient Egypt. Taylor Swift's "Love Story" **EVOKES** a time when beautiful princesses lived in romantic castles and fell in love with handsome princes. And the movie *Titanic* is a remarkable **EVOCATION** of what it was like to be a passenger on the great but doomed ship.

KNOW YOUR ROOTS		
LATIN ROOT: *VOC,* *VOK* | call	VOCAL	related to the voice, speaking
	VOCATION	your calling, your profession, often used for a religious career
	AVOCATION	a second calling, a hobby
	EVOKE	to call forth, especially from the past
	REVOKE	to call back, to rescind, to repeal
	INVOKE	to call upon. Epic poems often begin with an Invocation of the Muse, or goddess of artistic inspiration.
	PROVOKE	to call forth (see Word 82)
	CONVOCATION	a calling together, a gathering
	VOCIFEROUS	making an outcry, clamorous
	EQUIVOCATE	to use AMBIGUOUS (Word 21) expressions, to mislead
	IRREVOCABLE	incapable of being recalled or altered

14 | PRESUMPTUOUS

Taking liberties; brashly overstepping one's place; impertinently bold; displaying EFFRONTERY

One of the most **PRESUMPTUOUS** actions in recent memory occurred during the 2009 MTV Video Music Awards. When Taylor Swift came onstage to accept her award for her "You Belong With Me" video, Kanye West appeared and grabbed the microphone out of her hand. He **PRESUMPTUOUSLY** declared, "Taylor, I'm really happy for you. Imma let you finish, but Beyoncé had one of the best videos of all time!" His **AUDACIOUS** (Word 9) **EFFRONTERY** (rude, arrogant behavior) shocked Taylor, Beyoncé, and all who watched the VMAs, and he was widely criticized for it. Eventually, Kanye recognized how **PRESUMPTUOUS** his actions were and made a formal apology on *The Tonight Show with Jay Leno*.

15 | RECALCITRANT

Stubbornly resistant and defiant; OBSTINATE; OBDURATE; REFRACTORY (Word 421); disobedient

What do Hester Prynne (*The Scarlet Letter*) and the actor Charlie Sheen have in common? Both are **RECALCITRANT**. In *The Scarlet Letter*, the

Reverend Wilson demanded that Hester reveal the identity of the father of her child. But Hester was **RECALCITRANT**. Despite "the heavy weight of a thousand eyes, all fastened upon her," Hester stubbornly refused to name the father, defiantly declaring, "Never… I will not speak!"

When the producers of the show *Two and a Half Men* told Charlie Sheen that his drug abuse was a serious problem that could kill him, he **RECALCITRANTLY** responded, "I'm different. I have a different constitution, I have a different brain, I have a different heart. I got tiger blood, man. Dying's for fools, dying's for amateurs." A year after the **FIASCO** (Word 146), Sheen says he is no longer taking drugs, but he still **RECALCITRANTLY** refuses to stop drinking alcohol.

16 | BOON
A timely benefit; blessing

BANE
A source of harm and ruin

Fifty Cent was shot nine times and lived! Was the shooting a **BANE** or a **BOON** for his career? At first it was a **BANE** because he had to spend weeks in a hospital in excruciating pain. But the shooting turned out to be a **BOON** for his career because it **BOLSTERED** (reinforced) Fiddy's "street cred" and attracted lots of publicity.

In Shakespeare's *Othello*, the main character, Othello, fires his lieutenant, Cassio, for inappropriate behavior. Desdemona, Othello's wife, comes to plead for Cassio's reinstatement. She argues that she is not asking for a huge favor: "Why, this is not a **BOON**." She continues that he should instead just think of this request as something normal. Unfortunately for Cassio, the villain Iago is **SURREPTITIOUSLY** (Word 17) working to make Othello think that Desdemona and Cassio are having an affair, even though they are not. Othello, therefore, comes to believe that Cassio is the **BANE** of his existence.

17 | CLANDESTINE, SURREPTITIOUS
*Secret; covert; not open; NOT **ABOVEBOARD***

What do the Men in Black (*Men in Black*), Dumbledore's Army (*Harry Potter and the Order of the Phoenix*), and S.H.I.E.L.D. (*The Avengers*) all have in common? They are all **CLANDESTINE** groups that conduct **SURREPTITIOUS** activities. The Men in Black **SURREPTITIOUSLY** regulate alien life forms on Earth. Dumbledore's Army teaches Hogwarts students how to defend themselves against the Dark Arts. S.H.I.E.L.D. is a covert intelligence agency that **MARSHALS** (arrays for battle) the Avengers team to protect the world from superhuman threats.

18 | AFFABLE, AMIABLE, GENIAL, GREGARIOUS
Agreeable; marked by a pleasing personality; warm and friendly

President Reagan was renowned for his **AFFABLE** grace and **GENIAL** good humor. On March 6, 1981, a deranged gunman shot the president as he was leaving a Washington hotel. The injured but always **AMIABLE** president looked up at his doctors and nurses and said, "I hope you're all Republicans." The first words the President uttered upon regaining consciousness were to a nurse who happened to be holding his hand. "Does Nancy know about us?" the president joked.

KNOW YOUR ROOTS

The English word AMIABLE contains the Latin root *ami* meaning friend. You may have heard this root in the French word *ami* and the Spanish word *amigo*.

| LATIN ROOT: | AMITY | friendship, harmony |
| *AMI* \| friend | AMICABLE | peaceable, harmonious |

19 | AUSTERE
*Having no adornment or ornamentation; bare; not **ORNATE** (Word 397)*

AUSTERITY
Great self-denial, economy, discipline; lack of adornment

Ancient Greek architects often used Doric columns to construct temples. For example, the Parthenon's **AUSTERE** columns conveyed strength and simplicity because they lacked ornamentation.

Although modern Greeks admire the **AUSTERE** columns built by their ancestors, they vigorously oppose new **AUSTERITY** measures that raise taxes and cut social welfare programs. These **AUSTERITY** measures provoked massive protests.

20 | ALTRUISM
Unselfish concern for the welfare of others

The term was originally **COINED** (Word 296) in the 19th century by the sociologist and philosopher of science Auguste Comte. Comte referred to **ALTRUISM** as being the moral obligation of individuals to serve other people and to place others' interests above their own.

Mahatma Gandhi, Martin Luther King, Jr., and Mother Teresa are all people who exemplify **ALTRUISM** through their belief in the basic rights of all people regardless of race, creed, or social standing, and through their service and sacrifices for others.

Much **ALTRUISTIC** behavior was seen in the selfless actions of the first responders when the World Trade Center towers were attacked on 9/11.

21 | AMBIGUITY

The quality or state of having more than one possible meaning; doubtful; EQUIVOCAL (Word 215)

AMBIGUOUS

Unclear; uncertain; open to more than one interpretation; not definitive; DUBIOUS

The final scene of the movie *Inception* is full of **AMBIGUITY**. Leo DiCaprio's character, Dom Cobb, is **ELATED** (very happy) because he has found his children and completed the seemingly impossible job he was hired to do. But is all this real or is Dom entrapped in yet another dream? Dom uses a metal top to enable him to determine what is real and what isn't. At the end of the film, Dom spins the top. What will happen next? If the top keeps spinning, Dom is dreaming. If it falls, things are real. We don't know what happens because the ending is deliberately **AMBIGUOUS** (See KNOW YOUR ROOTS, p. 2).

22 | UPBRAID, REPROACH, CASTIGATE

To express disapproval; to scold; to rebuke; to CENSURE

In this classic scene from *Billy Madison*, Ms. Vaughn **UPBRAIDS** Billy for making fun of a third grade student who is having trouble reading:

Third Grader:	Wa-wa-wa-once th-th-th-th-there wa-wa-wa-was a-a-a-a g-g-girl
Billy Madison:	Kid can't even read.
Ernie:	Cut it out, dude, you're gonna get us in trouble.
Billy Madison:	T-T-T-Today Junior!
Billy Madison:	OW! You're tearing my ear off!
Veronica Vaughn:	Making fun of a little kid for trying to read. Are you psycho? Do you not have a soul? You keep your mouth shut for the next two weeks or I'm going to fail you. End of story.

23 | NOSTALGIA

*A **WISTFUL** (Word 206) sentimental longing for a place or time in the past*

A lifelong fan of The Muppets, Jason Segel was **NOSTALGIC** for his childhood, and he decided to **REJUVENATE** (Word 171) the franchise by writing a new movie for them. Segel said, "We set out to make a Muppet movie that harkened back to the late-'70s, early-'80s Muppets that we grew up with." It's been over a decade since The Muppets starred in a theatrical movie, and, likewise, in *The Muppets*, it's been a while since Kermit and his friends have performed as a group. As the audience revisits their childhood icons during this **NOSTALGIC** film, The Muppets, too, take a **WISTFUL** (Word 206) walk down memory lane. The Muppets decide to get their group together again for one last show, but they discover that they aren't popular anymore. They have become **ANTIQUATED** (Word 25); one character tells them, "You're **RELICS** (surviving objects from the past)." By incorporating clever humor and **WISTFUL** (Word 206) references to Muppet movies of the past, *The Muppets* introduces a new generation to the **WHIMSICAL** (Word 219) world of Kermit and his friends while also catering to an older **DEMOGRAPHIC's** (Word 433) **NOSTALGIA** for their childhood.

24 | CONJECTURE

*An inference based upon guesswork; a **SUPPOSITION***

What caused the sudden extinction of the dinosaurs? Scientists have offered a number of **CONJECTURES** to explain why the Age of Dinosaurs came to an abrupt end. One popular **CONJECTURE** suggests that a giant meteor struck Mexico's Yucatan Peninsula, causing widespread firestorms, tidal waves, and the severe downpour of acid rain. An alternative **CONJECTURE** suggests that massive volcanic eruptions at the Deccan Flats in India caused climate changes that killed the dinosaurs. While both **CONJECTURES** are **PLAUSIBLE** (Word 38), scientists still lack a definitive explanation.

25 | OBSOLETE, ARCHAIC, ANTIQUATED
No longer in use; outmoded in design or style

For many years Kodak was the **ICONIC** (idolized as an object of attention or devotion) leader in the photo industry. Many of its products became **ANTIQUATED** and, in the case of camera film, nearly **OBSOLETE**. Kodak's **MYOPIC** (shortsighted, lacking foresight) business model caused them to be late in entering the successor market—digital photography.

26 | AUSPICIOUS, PROPITIOUS
Very favorable

How long would you wait to marry your true love? The Mogul princes of India were required to wait until the emperor's astrologers felt that all of the planetary signs were **AUSPICIOUS**. For example, they required Crown Prince Shah Jahan and Mumtaz Mahal to postpone their wedding date for five years. During that time, the lovers were not allowed to see one another. The long-awaited wedding finally took place when all of the astrological signs were **AUSPICIOUS**. The signs must have indeed been **PROPITIOUS** because the royal couple enjoyed 19 years of marital joy and happiness.

27 | GAFFE
A blunder; a faux pas; *a clumsy social or diplomatic error*

The 2012 Olympic Games provided their share of **GAFFES**. Just before the soccer events began, it was learned that the keys to Wembley Stadium had been lost, forcing officials to hastily change all the locks. It appears that the keys had not been stolen, just misplaced.

Then the North Korean women's soccer team walked off the field at their opening match when organizers mistakenly introduced the players displaying South Korea's flag on the stadium screens. This was a serious *faux pas*: the two countries are still technically at war. Only after more than an hour's coaxing, **ABJECT** (humble) apologies, and the replacement of South Korea's largely white flag with images of North

Korea's red banner did the offended North Korean women agree to take the field.

Another embarrassing blunder occurred when the New Zealand Olympic Committee forgot to register the defending champion Valerie Adams for the shot put. The **GAFFE** was spotted before it was too late, and her name was added to the roster.

28 | IMPASSE
A deadlock; stalemate; failure to reach an agreement

In *The Hunger Games*, the Gamemakers change the rules and announce that two tributes from the same district may win the competition together, so District 12 tributes Katniss and Peeta team up to defeat the others. When they are the only remaining tributes, the Gamemakers **RESCIND** (revoke) the previous rule change and say that only one of them can win in the deadly competition. In response, Katniss takes some poisonous berries from her pouch and shares them with Peeta; they intend to eat the berries together rather than fight each other. Katniss and Peeta are at an **IMPASSE** with the Gamemakers. They would rather die together than fight, and the Gamemakers want only one victor. Finally, the Gamemakers are **COERCED** (Word 273) into allowing both victors because of Katniss and Peeta's suicide threat. They would rather have two winners than none.

29 | ANACHRONISM
The false assignment of an event, person, scene, or language to a time when the event, person, scene, or word did not exist

Northern Renaissance artists often included **ANACHRONISMS** in their paintings. For example, *Last Supper* by the 15th century artist Dirk Bouts shows Christ and his disciples eating in a royal palace in what is today Belgium. While the **ANACHRONISM** in Bouts's painting is deliberate, the **ANACHRONISMS** in modern movies are unplanned blunders. For example, in the Civil War movie *Glory*, a digital watch is clearly visible on the wrist of a boy waving goodbye to the black soldiers of the

54th Massachusetts Regiment. And in the movie *Gladiator*, you can see a gas cylinder in the back of one of the overturned "Roman" chariots!

KNOW YOUR ROOTS		
GREEK ROOT: ***CHRONO*** | time	CHRONOLOGY	the science of recording events by date
	CHRONIC	continuing for a long time
	SYNCHRONIC	happening at the same time
	SYNCHRONICITY	phenomenon of events which coincide in time and appear meaningfully related but have no discoverable causal connection
	SYNCHRONIZE	to cause to go at the same rate or occur at the same time (as a timepiece or a schedule)
	CHRONICLE	a record of events in order of time
	CHRONICLER	an historian, as a chronicler of events

30 | BELIE

To contradict; to prove false, used of appearances that are misrepresentative

In *Catching Fire*, the second installment of *The Hunger Games* **SAGA** (Word 236), Katniss and Peeta are forced to return to the arena for the Quarter Quell, a special 75th edition of the Hunger Games, in which they must compete against other previous victors of the Games. They form alliances with several of the other tributes, including Wiress, an **ECCENTRIC** (Word 157) woman from District 3 who rarely speaks in complete sentences. Her **UNCONVENTIONAL** (Word 7) and seemingly unbalanced behavior has earned her the nickname "Nuts." However, her unusual behavior **BELIES** an extraordinary intelligence and intuition. She becomes a strong asset to the team, figures out crucial information concerning the arena's design, and helps her allies survive in the dangerous environment of the Games.

31 | MITIGATE, MOLLIFY, ASSUAGE, ALLEVIATE
To relieve; to lessen; to ease

Did you know that almost half of all Americans take at least one prescription pill every day? Americans use pills to **ALLEVIATE** the symptoms of everything from migraine headaches to acid indigestion.

Stephen Douglas believed that the doctrine of popular sovereignty would **MITIGATE**, or lessen, the public's passions against the extension of slavery into the territories. But Douglas badly misjudged the public mood in the North. Instead of **MOLLIFYING** the public, popular sovereignty inflamed passions and helped propel the nation toward the Civil War.

32 | COVET
To strongly desire; to crave

COVETOUS
Grasping, greedy, eager to obtain something; AVARICIOUS (Word 255)

What do Lord Voldemort (*Harry Potter and the Deathly Hallows*), The Wicked Witch of the West (*Wizard of Oz*), and Megatron (*Transformers*) all have in common? All three villains are **COVETOUS** of something they desperately want but can't have. Lord Voldemort **COVETS** the Elder Wand, the Wicked Witch of the West **COVETS** Dorothy's Ruby Slippers, and Megatron **COVETS** the All Spark.

33 | ANTITHESIS
The direct or exact opposite; extreme contrast; ANTIPODE

ANTITHETICAL
Exactly opposite; ANTIPODAL

In her song "You Belong With Me," Taylor Swift cannot **FATHOM** (understand) why a guy she likes continues to go out with a girl who is his complete **ANTITHESIS**. Their tastes in music and sense of humor are **ANTITHETICAL**. But Taylor recognizes that her rival is a cheer captain who "wears short skirts" while Taylor sits in the bleachers and "wears t-shirts." All Taylor can do is hope that the guy will have an **EPIPHANY** (Word 327) and realize that they belong together.

34 | PROTOTYPE
An original model; an initial design

What do the Model T and The Bat in *The Dark Knight Rises* have in common? Although very different vehicles, both were originally designed to be **PROTOTYPES**. The Model T, invented by Henry Ford in 1908, served as the **PROTOTYPE** for the world's first affordable, mass-produced automobile. The Bat, created by Lucius Fox at Wayne Enterprises, was a **PROTOTYPE** for a flying tank military vehicle, but it helped Batman save Gotham from Bane and his men.

35 | ALOOF
Detached; distant physically or emotionally; reserved; standing near but apart

In *The Great Gatsby*, Fitzgerald initially portrays Jay Gatsby as the **ALOOF** host of lavish parties given every week at his **ORNATE** (Word 397) mansion. Although he is courted by powerful men and beautiful women, Gatsby chooses to remain distant and **ALOOF**.

In Homer's *Iliad*, many people accused Zeus of "wanting to give victory to the Trojans." But Zeus chose to remain **ALOOF**: "He sat apart in his all-glorious majesty, looking down upon the Trojans, the ships of the Achaeans, the gleam of bronze, and alike upon the slayers and the slain."

36 | TRITE, HACKNEYED, BANAL, PLATITUDINOUS, INSIPID
Unoriginal; commonplace; overused; CLICHÉD

In *The Catcher in the Rye*, Holden Caulfield just can't help seeing most people as "phony"—his favorite word. When he goes to hear Ernie, the jazz piano player, he thinks of the playing as **BANAL**: so lacking in originality that it is almost boring. He sees straight through his headmaster's **PLATITUDE** that "Life is a game," understanding the message to be **TRITE**, unoriginal, and lacking freshness. Many people who read *The Catcher in the Rye* today think of Holden Caulfield's very character as **HACKNEYED**, because he represents a character we have seen all too many times: the moody, **DISAFFECTED** (disconnected), disgruntled teenager. But back in 1951, when the novel was first published, Salinger's portrait of a young person was considered **SEARINGLY** (scorchingly) original.

Paula Abdul, the former *American Idol* and *X-Factor* judge, was known for being nice and **AFFABLE** (Word 18), always saying something positive to the contestants. Although Paula was nice, her comments were **TRITE**, **BANAL**, and **HACKNEYED**. According to **PLATITUDINOUS** Paula, every singer was "great," "beautiful," and "amazing." She encouraged each one with pleasant but **INSIPID** compliments like "You're authentic," "America loves you," and "Your journey of magic is just beginning."

37 | ANTECEDENT
A preceding event; a FORERUNNER; a PRECURSOR

Many critics have noted that the 1995 Disney movie *Pocahontas* can be viewed as a thematic **ANTECEDENT** to the 2010 blockbuster *Avatar*. In *Pocahontas*, **AVARICIOUS** (Word 255) English settlers search for gold. In *Avatar*, an **AVARICIOUS** company wants to mine unobtanium from the fictional planet Pandora. In both movies beautiful **INDIGENOUS** (Word 47) women rescue soldiers who find themselves drawn to the native peoples they originally intended to conquer. By helping Captain John Smith discover the New World's life and beauty, Pocahontas serves as an **ANTECEDENT** for Avatar's Neytiri.

KNOW YOUR ROOTS		
GREEK PREFIX: **ANTE** | before	ANTEBELLUM	before the Civil War
	ANTEDILUVIAN	before the Biblical flood, a hyperbolic word describing something extremely old
	ANTEDATE	to precede in time
	ANTEROOM	a waiting room outside a larger room
	ANTERIOR	before in time and place

38 | PLAUSIBLE
Believable; credible

IMPLAUSIBLE
Unbelievable; incredible

Let's play **PLAUSIBLE** or **IMPLAUSIBLE**:

In the *Bourne Ultimatum*, Jason Bourne successfully breaks into Noah Vosen's heavily-guarded top-security office and steals an entire set of classified Blackbriar documents. **PLAUSIBLE** or **IMPLAUSIBLE**? **PLAUSIBLE**—because he is Jason Bourne!

In *The Avengers*, Iron Man, Captain America, Thor, The Hulk, Hawkeye, and Black Widow successfully save New York City from an extraterrestrial attack and a nuclear missile. **PLAUSIBLE** or **IMPLAUSIBLE**? **PLAUSIBLE**—because The Avengers all have special skills and powers that allow them to defeat their foes!

39 | PRUDENT
Careful; cautious; sensible

In the *Twilight* **SAGA** (Word 236), Bella Swan is a high school student who meets and falls in love with Edward Cullen. However, Edward is not just another high school student. He is a 107-year-old vampire who stopped aging physically at 17. Edward understands that their relationship poses grave dangers to Bella. However, Bella and Edward love each other, so they decide to stay together despite the danger. Together, they must be **PRUDENT** in dealing with the dangers that they face, among them werewolves, vengeful vampires, and the **OMINOUS** (Word 197) Volturi.

40 | AESTHETIC

Relating to the nature of beauty, art, and taste; having a sense of what is beautiful, attractive, or pleasing

Do you know why the *Mona Lisa* is considered one of the most beautiful paintings of all time? The answer lies in its use of the Golden Ratio, the naturally occurring ratio of height to width that is most **AESTHETICALLY** pleasing to humans. The *Mona Lisa*'s face is composed entirely of Golden Ratio rectangles and thus adds to the overall **AESTHETIC** of the painting. However, the Golden Ratio is not limited to art. Examples can be found in ancient Greek architecture, Egyptian pyramids, biology, and even widescreen television screens!

It is not **AESTHETICALLY** pleasing if a character introduced at the very end solves a novel or play's conflicts. Aristotle criticized Euripides' play *Medea* for having Medea saved at the end by a character not integral to the plot. To his mind, **AESTHETICALLY** this was not a satisfying conclusion.

41 | PARADOX

A seemingly contradictory statement that nonetheless expresses a truth

One of the most famous literary first lines is that of Charles Dickens's *A Tale of Two Cities*: "It was the best of times, it was the worst of times." How could such a contradiction be true? In the course of the book, this **PARADOXICAL** statement is shown to be valid.

In Mary Shelley's novel *Frankenstein*, the creature encounters many **PARADOXES**. One is the simultaneous positive and negative characteristics of fire. It can warm him, protect him, light his way, and cook his food, but it can also burn and destroy. Similarly, the creature also comes to recognize the **PARADOXICAL** nature of man: driven by conflicting forces of selfishness and **ALTRUISM** (Word 20).

42 | ENIGMATIC, INSCRUTABLE
Mysterious; puzzling; unfathomable; baffling

What do Da Vinci's *Mona Lisa*, Fitzgerald's description of Jay Gatsby, and J.K. Rowling's portrayal of Snape have in common? All three figures are **ENIGMATIC**. The *Mona Lisa's* **ENIGMATIC** smile has puzzled art lovers for centuries. When *The Great Gatsby* opens, Jay Gatsby is an **ENIGMATIC** figure whose great wealth and extravagant parties spark endless gossip. And Snape's personality and loyalties remain **INSCRUTABLE** until the final chapters of *Harry Potter and the Deathly Hallows*.

43 | ACQUIESCE
To comply; to agree; to give in

In *Pirates of the Caribbean: The Curse of the Black Pearl*, Elizabeth Swann and Captain Barbossa conduct negotiations that include long words.

Elizabeth Swann: Captain Barbossa, I am here to negotiate the cessation of hostilities against Port Royal.

Captain Barbossa: There be a lot of long words in there, Miss. We're naught but humble pirates. What is it that you want?

Elizabeth Swann: I want you to leave and never come back.

Captain Barbossa: I'm disinclined to **ACQUIESCE** to your request. Means no!

Although he is a "humble pirate," Captain Barbossa can use long words as well as she can.

44 | NAÏVE, GULLIBLE
Unaffectedly simple; lacking worldly expertise; overly CREDULOUS; unsophisticated; immature; inexperienced; INGENUOUS (Word 428)

Nemo, of *Finding Nemo*, is a young clown fish who thinks he is old enough to swim out in the open waters. Young, **NAÏVE**, and wanting to defy his overprotective father, he wanders too near a boat. Suddenly, a net surrounds him. He is taken aboard the boat and from there to Sydney, Australia, to live in a fish tank. His father Marlin, **DESPONDENT** (Word 176) at his loss, vows to find his son. Marlin succeeds and ultimately brings Nemo back home. By the end of the film, Nemo has learned the importance of obeying his father and of not being so **GULLIBLE**.

45 | AUTONOMY
Independence; self-governance

AUTONOMOUS
Acting independently, or having the freedom to do so; not controlled by others

Fahrenheit 451, the classic novel by Ray Bradbury, imagines a **DYSTOPIA** (an imaginery society characterized by oppression and human misery) society in which a faceless government exerts huge control over its citizens.   No books are allowed; instead, citizens watch endless television streams of **PROPAGANDA** (zealous advancement of a group's principles) from the government. Bradbury's novel suggests that people naturally desire **AUTONOMY** in their own lives; if a faceless government tries to exert authority over them, they will tend to be **SUBVERSIVE** (tending to overthrow), and rebel against that authority.

In the movie *Men in Black*, Agent Zed explains that MIB is an **AUTONOMOUS** organization that is "not a part of the system." He goes on to say that MIB is "above the system, over it, beyond it; we are they, we are them, we are the Men in Black." They are serious about their **AUTONOMY**!

46 | FUTILE
Completely useless; doomed to failure; in vain

The Deepwater Horizon oil spill released a **PRODIGIOUS** (huge, massive) flood of crude oil into the Gulf of Mexico. BP engineers made repeated attempts to control or stop the spill. However, all of their initial efforts proved to be **FUTILE**. Although crews worked tirelessly to protect hundreds of miles of beaches, wetlands, and estuaries, local residents worried that these efforts would also prove to be **FUTILE**.

47 | INDIGENOUS, ENDEMIC
Native to an area

Which of the following are Old World plants and animals, and which are New World plants and animals: potatoes, tomatoes, maize, sunflowers, cocoa beans, turkeys, and buffaloes? Surprisingly, all of these plants and animals are **INDIGENOUS** or **ENDEMIC** to the New World!

KNOW YOUR ROOTS		
GREEK ROOT: ***DEM,*** the people ***DEMO***	PANDEMIC (Word 49)	of all the people, prevalent over a whole area
	DEMOCRACY	rule by the people, by the majority
	DEMAGOGUE (Word 111)	a person who tries to stir up the people by appealing to emotion and prejudice in order to achieve selfish ends
	DEMOGRAPHICS (Word 433)	the science of vital statistics about populations (births, deaths, marriages, incomes, etc.)
	EPIDEMIC	a rapid spread of a contagious disease or other negative condition

48 | UBIQUITOUS, PREVALENT
Characterized by being everywhere; omnipresent; widespread; PERVASIVE

What do cell phones, iPods, Starbucks coffee shops, and McDonald's fast-food restaurants have in common? They are all **UBIQUITOUS**— we see them everywhere. Popular fashions are also **PERVASIVE**. For example, baggy knee-length shorts have completely replaced the once-**PREVALENT** short shorts of the 1970s. From high school b-ballers to WNBA and NBA superstars, long shorts are now **UBIQUITOUS**.

49 | PANDEMIC

An epidemic that is geographically widespread and affects a large proportion of the population

In the movie *I Am Legend*, a manmade virus known as KV triggers a global **PANDEMIC** that kills almost all of the human population on Earth. While there has never been a real **PANDEMIC** of this magnitude, virus strains and diseases have caused widespread deaths. In 1347 the Black Plague killed as many as one-third of the people in Europe. In the 16th century, Spanish conquistadores spread small pox and other diseases that **DECIMATED** (destroyed a great proportion of) the **INDIGENOUS** (Word 47) populations in Central America, the Caribbean, and Mexico. Our own times have not been immune to epidemics. The 1918 flu **PANDEMIC** killed 50 to 100 million people, and more recently we have had SARS, Asian Bird Flu, and Swine Flu **PANDEMICS**.

PANDEMIC can also be used as an adjective, meaning **PREVALENT** (Word 48) over a large area.

50 | FORTITUDE

Strength of mind that allows one to endure pain or adversity with courage

William Lloyd Garrison and Rosa Parks demonstrated great personal **FORTITUDE**. While most Americans accepted slavery, Garrison boldly demanded the immediate and unconditional emancipation of all slaves. Although initially ignored, Garrison **PERSEVERED** (refused to give up no matter the situation) and lived to see President Lincoln issue the Emancipation Proclamation. Rosa Parks also illustrates the principle that **FORTITUDE** is needed to achieve difficult goals. While most Americans accepted segregation, Rosa refused a bus driver's order to give up her seat to a white passenger. Her historic action helped **GALVANIZE** (Word 148) the Civil Rights Movement.

CHAPTER 2

Core Vocabulary II | *51 – 100*

Chapter 2 continues to build the list of 100 Core Vocabulary Words. As in Chapter 1, each of these words has been the key to a Level 3 or Level 4 question. We **EXHORT** (Word 53) you to study hard. As always, our **PENCHANT** (Word 62) for vivid pop culture examples will help you learn and remember new words. So don't let the Core Words **THWART** (Word 67) you. Now is the time to **TENACIOUSLY** (Word 56) pursue your goal of conquering the SAT. Remember, there is **INCONTROVERTIBLE** (Word 70) proof that your Critical Reading score will go up as your vocabulary goes up!

51 | DIMINUTIVE
Very small

The 2012 Summer Olympics coverage featured the latest team of **DIMINUTIVE** gymnasts, five American girls who averaged 16 years old, 5'1" tall, and 104 pounds, and who performed astounding feats of strength, agility, and precision. Led by Gabby Douglas, who also took first place in the individual all-around event, the **DIMINUTIVE** Fab Five brought home the women's team gold medal for the first time since 1996. Gabby, at 4'11' and 90 pounds the most **DIMINUTIVE** of the bunch, was dubbed "the flying squirrel" by Marta Karolyi, the U.S. national team coordinator. Given the rigors of the intense training, the high incidence of injuries, and the other sacrifices required in order to reach the highest level of the sport, women gymnasts have a short shelf life. But in August 2012, **DIMINUTIVE** Gabby Douglas won the hearts of Americans everywhere.

52 | TRIVIAL
Trifling; unimportant; insignificant
MINUTIAE
Minor everyday details

Drake is one of the world's most popular hip hop artists. While Drake would prefer to concentrate on creating music, his zealous fans often focus on interesting but **TRIVIAL MINUTIAE** about his personal life. For example, Drake was raised by a Jewish mother and had a Bar Mitzvah. And online rumors continue to link him with Rihanna!

53 | EXHORT
To encourage; to urge; to give a pep talk; to IMPLORE

American League baseball player Derek Jeter has spent his entire career with the New York Yankees. Naturally, New York fans love him. When Jeter began to approach the **COVETED** (Word 32) 3,000 hit milestone, his teammates and fans **EXHORTED** him to continue to play well so he could reach the **ELUSIVE** (Word 161) milestone. The **EXHORTATIONS** worked. On July 9, 2011 he became the first New York Yankee to reach the 3,000 hit mark. Even sweeter, his 3,000th hit was a home run!

54 | ANTIPATHY

Strong dislike; ill will; the state of DETESTING someone; ENMITY; RANCOR

In *The Social Network,* Cameron and Tyler Winklevoss and their business partner, Divya Narendra, approached Mark Zuckerberg with an idea they called "HarvardConnection," an online social network exclusively for Harvard University students and alumni.

Zuckerberg broke his agreement with the HarvardConnection team and approached his friend Eduardo Saverin about a nearly identical website idea called "Thefacebook." The first website to allow the entire campus to communicate and socialize with ease, Thefacebook skyrocketed in popularity.

Can you imagine the **ANTIPATHY** that the Winklevoss brothers and Narendra felt upon seeing their idea becoming successful without them? In the movie scene, Narendra discovered Zuckerberg's Thefacebook, slammed his laptop closed, and, filled with **ENMITY**, stormed out of the room to inform the Winklevoss brothers of Zuckerberg's betrayal.

55 | DIGRESS

To depart from a subject; to wander; to ramble

Have you ever listened to someone who repeatedly wanders off a topic? If so, then you know how confusing and annoying it is when a speaker **DIGRESSES** from a subject. In the movie *Office Space*, Milton is **NOTORIOUS** (widely but unfavorably known) for his long-winded **DIGRESSIONS**. **DIGRESSING** is not limited to speaking. Writers sometimes **DIGRESS** or wander off a topic. On the SAT I, your first task will be to write an essay. Readers reward essays that are well-organized and deduct points from essays that **DIGRESS** from the topic.

KNOW YOUR ROOTS

LATIN ROOT: ***GRESS*** | to step	PROGRESS	to step forward
	REGRESS	to step back
	TRANSGRESS	to step across the line that divides right from wrong
	EGRESS	to step out, to exit (or as a noun, an exit)
	AGGRESSIVE	tending to attack, encroach, or step on others

---

56 | TENACIOUS

Characterized by holding fast to something valued; showing great determination

Tip for a Direct Hit

The root of TENACIOUS is the Latin root *TEN*, "to hold." You can find it in TENET, an opinion, idea, or principle HELD true by a person or organization. It's also in TENABLE, which means capable of being HELD, defended, and logically supported, as in a TENABLE argument or thesis.

The 2006 film *Amazing Grace* tells the story of the 20-year campaign against the British slave trade led by the **TENACIOUS** Member of Parliament William Wilberforce. Through Wilberforce's **TENACITY** and determination, the battle **CULMINATED** (reached completion) in the 1807 bill that abolished the slave trade in the British Empire. Though the film is not totally accurate historically, it does make the inspiring point of the effectiveness of sheer **TENACITY** in the face of almost impossible odds.

Think too about the **TENACITY** of a dog with a bone, never letting go. That might remind you of the word **DOGGED** (pronounced with two syllables), which means having the **TENACITY** of a dog. You can also use **TENACIOUSNESS** instead of **TENACITY**; they mean the same thing.

57 | INDULGENT

Characterized by excessive generosity; overly tolerant

In the movie *Mean Girls*, Regina George's mother prides herself on being **INDULGENT**. She proudly tells Regina and Cady, "I just want you to know, if you ever need anything, don't be shy, OK? There are NO rules in the house. I'm not like a 'regular' mom. I'm a 'cool' mom." Mrs. George should have said, "I'm a super-**INDULGENT** mom who lets Regina do anything she wishes."

58 | POLARIZE

To create disunity or dissension; to break up into opposing factions or groups; to be DIVISIVE

Americans have a long and distinguished record of settling differences by reaching a compromise. However, some issues are so **DIVISIVE** and **POLARIZING** that a compromise is impossible. Before the Civil War, the issue of slavery **POLARIZED** Americans into two groups: those who defended the South's "peculiar institution" and those who demanded that slavery be abolished. As Lincoln eloquently noted: "A house divided against itself cannot stand. I believe this government cannot endure permanently half slave and half free."

59 | NEBULOUS

Vague; cloudy; misty; lacking a fully-developed form

Have you read the Epilogue in *Harry Potter and the Deathly Hallows*? If you found it rather vague, then J.K. Rowling achieved her goal. In an interview, Rowling stated that the Epilogue is deliberately "**NEBULOUS**." She wanted readers to feel as if they were looking at Platform 9 3/4 through the mist, unable to make out exactly who was there and who was not.

60 | ANALOGY

A similarity or likeness between things—events, ideas, actions, trends—that are otherwise unrelated

ANALOGOUS

Comparable or similar in certain respects

Did you know that for most of its history the SAT included a number of **ANALOGY** questions? For example, students were asked to see the

ANALOGY or similarity between a tree and a forest and a star and a galaxy. The **ANALOGY** is that a tree is part of a forest in the same way that a star is part of a galaxy. Although the College Board removed analogies in 2005, SAT test writers still expect students to recognize **ANALOGIES** in critical readings. Don't be confused by the phrase "is most **ANALOGOUS** to." The question is asking you to identify a situation or example that is most similar to the one in the reading passage.

61 | EPHEMERAL, FLEETING, EVANESCENT

Very brief; lasting for a short time; transient

PERENNIAL

Returning year after year; enduring

What do the following groups and their hit songs have in common: "Who Let the Dogs Out?" by Baha Men, "Stuck In The Middle With You" by Stealers Wheel, and "It's Raining Men" by the Weather Girls? All three groups were "one-hit wonders" who had a single hit song and then disappeared. Their popularity was **EVANESCENT**. They were **EPHEMERAL**—here today and gone tomorrow.

On the contrary, bands like The Beatles, The Beach Boys, and Simon & Garfunkel have remained **PERENNIAL** favorites. The Beatles' albums continue to be bestsellers on iTunes. The Beach Boys still maintain a busy tour schedule, and the songs of Simon & Garfunkel remain staples of popular culture. Paul Simon was even asked to perform their hit song "The Sound of Silence" at the 9/11 tenth anniversary memorial service. All three of these bands have maintained immense popularity throughout the decades.

62 | PENCHANT, PREDILECTION, PROPENSITY

A liking or preference for something; a BENT (Word 299);
an INCLINATION

What do film star Angelina Jolie and rap artist Lil Wayne have in common? Both have a well-known **PENCHANT** for tattoos. Angelina's tattoos include a prayer of Buddhist Sanskrit symbols to honor her first adopted son, Maddox, coordinates representing the geographic locations of her children's birthplaces, and the statement "know your rights." Lil Wayne's **PREDILECTION** for tattoos has led him to cover his face and torso with tattoos. For example, a red tattoo above his right eyebrow states, "I am music," emphasizing his love of music. The numbers 9 27 82 on his right forearm are his date of birth.

63 | CAPRICIOUS, MERCURIAL, FICKLE
Very changeable; characterized by constantly-shifting moods

When the gossip magazine *Us Weekly* published a story and photos of *Twilight*'s Kristen Stewart cheating on her boyfriend Robert Pattinson, passionate *Twilight* fans responded in disbelief on their Twitter accounts. The outraged fans **LAMBASTED** (Word 310) the magazine and insisted that the photos of Stewart were fake. However, Stewart released a statement apologizing for her "momentary indiscretion" and declaring her love for Pattinson. The **FICKLE** fans turned **CAPRICIOUSLY** from supporting Stewart to **CASTIGATING** (severely criticizing) her and mourning the end of their favorite celebrity couple. Fans added **MAUDLIN** (Word 142) videos and social media posts online, **BEMOANING** (to express grief over) the breakup of "Robsten."

MEDIEVAL HUMOURS

In medieval times, it was believed that people's personalities or moods were determined by the relative amounts of the four bodily fluids (or HUMOURS) in their bodies. Though we no longer believe in the physiological basis, we still use the words to describe people.

Predominant Fluid	Temperament	Aspects
Blood	SANGUINE	cheerful, hopeful, optimistic
Black bile	MELANCHOLY	gloomy, depressed, DESPONDENT, PENSIVE
Yellow bile	CHOLERIC	angry, irritable, IRASCIBLE
Phlegm	PHLEGMATIC	self-possessed, imperturbable, calm, APATHETIC, sluggish
Fluctuating among all four fluids	MERCURIAL	volatile, changeable, FICKLE

64 | BOORISH, UNCOUTH, CRASS

Vulgar; characterized by crude behavior and deplorable manners; unrefined

Billy Madison (*Billy Madison*), Ron Burgundy (*Anchorman*), Borat (*Borat*), and Ben Stone (*Knocked Up*) all demonstrated **BOORISH** manners and behaviors. However, none of these **UNCOUTH** characters quite equaled Bluto in *Animal House*. In a classic scene, Bluto piled food onto his cafeteria plate while stuffing food in his pockets. He then sat down uninvited at a cafeteria table. Disgusted by Bluto's outrageous appearance and **CRASS** manners, Mandy called him a "P-I-G, pig." Undeterred by Mandy's insult, Bluto stuffed mashed potatoes into his mouth and asked Mandy and her **INCREDULOUS** (Word 363) friends, "See if you can guess what I am now." He then pressed his hands against his cheeks, causing the mashed potatoes to spray onto the shocked diners. Pleased with his **BOORISH** antics, Bluto proudly answered his own question by announcing, "I'm a zit! Get it?"

65 | INDIGNANT

Characterized by outrage at something that is perceived as unjust

What do Andrew Jackson's supporters in 1824 and Al Gore's supporters in 2000 have in common? Both were **INDIGNANT** at the outcomes of presidential elections. Following the election of 1824, Andrew Jackson's **INDIGNANT** supporters accused John Quincy Adams and Henry Clay of stealing the election from Old Hickory. Following the election of 2000, Al Gore's **INDIGNANT** supporters accused George W. Bush and the U.S. Supreme Court of stealing the election from Gore.

66 | INNUENDO

A veiled reference; an insinuation

At the beginning of *The Godfather*, Kay does not understand the workings of the Corleone family business, and she asks Michael how his father managed a business deal. Michael responds with an **INNUENDO**: "My father made him an offer he couldn't refuse." His response insinuates that Don Vito uses coercion and threats in his business dealings. Michael's **INNUENDO** suggests that his father is a powerful mob boss.

67 | THWART, STYMIE
To stop; to frustrate; to prevent

In the Harry Potter **SAGA** (Word 236) Lilly Potter's love **THWARTED** Lord Voldemort's attempt to kill her one-year-old son, Harry. With the help of Ron and Hermione, Harry repeatedly **THWARTED** the Dark Lord's attempts to kill him.

At the Paris Peace Conference at the end of World War I, which **CULMINATED** (concluded) in the Treaty of Versailles, most of President Woodrow Wilson's proposals for a "Just Peace" were **THWARTED** by the other world leaders, who were more interested in **RETRIBUTION** (punishment, vengeance). They did approve his plan for a League of Nations, which he hoped would be able to prevent future wars. When Wilson presented the treaty to the U.S. Senate, there was much opposition. The treaty went down to defeat, Wilson's efforts were again **STYMIED**, and the weak League of Nations never achieved its goals, lacking the participation of the world's newest superpower.

After the **CHICANERY** (Word 339) that came to light in 2011, new security measures have been implemented by both the SAT and the ACT to **STYMIE** those who might wish to take an exam for someone else. Students will now be required to upload a photo of themselves when registering for these exams. The photos will appear on the students' admission tickets and on the test site rosters available to proctors. Then the photos will be attached to any score reports sent to high schools and colleges.

68 | ADROIT, DEFT, ADEPT

*Having or showing great skill; **DEXTEROUS**; nimble*

Tip for a Direct Hit

Are you right-handed or left-handed? Right-handed people were once thought to be more ADROIT and DEXTEROUS than left-handed people. This bias can be seen in the etymology of these two words. The English word ADROIT is actually derived from the French word *droit* meaning right, as opposed to left. So if you are MALADROIT, you are not skillful. The ancient Romans shared the same positive view of right-handed people. The Latin word *dexter* means right, as opposed to left.

What do 16-year-old Austin Wierschke and action star Chuck Norris have in common? Austin has **DEXTEROUS** hands, and Chuck has **ADROIT** legs. Austin won the U.S. National Texting Championship two years in a row. He beat out 11 other finalists by **DEFTLY** texting blindfolded, texting with his hands behind his back, and by enduring rounds of marathon texting. As everyone knows, Chuck Norris is **ADEPT** at using a roundhouse kick to escape even the toughest situations. In fact, it is rumored that if someone were **DEFT** enough to harness the energy from a Chuck Norris roundhouse kick, he or she could power the entire country of Australia for 44 minutes.

69 | ADMONISH

To earnestly caution; to warn another to avoid a course of action

First sung in November 1934, "Santa Claus is Coming to Town" celebrates Santa's much-anticipated arrival on Christmas Eve. However, while Santa may be very **MUNIFICENT** (Word 258), he is also very **VIGILANT** (watchful, alert). He keeps a list, and he knows "who's naughty or nice." The song earnestly **ADMONISHES** children to "be good for goodness sake."

KNOW YOUR ROOTS		
LATIN ROOT: ***MON*** | to warn, remind	ADMONITION	a warning or reproof, a reminder
	PREMONITION	a warning in advance, PRESENTIMENT (hint) of something evil, foreboding
	MONITOR	a person or a device that reminds or checks (like a study hall monitor, a heart monitor, or an audio monitor for performers on a stage)
	MONUMENT	a sepulchre, memorial , edifice to commemorate something or someone notable, something that reminds (literally)

70 | INCONTROVERTIBLE
Impossible to deny or disprove; demonstrably true

In recent years the global warming debate has grown increasingly heated (no pun intended), politicized, and **POLARIZED** (Word 58). Al Gore's film, *An Inconvenient Truth*, presented statistics that many people challenge. But it is becoming clear that global warming is an **INCONTROVERTIBLE** fact. What is less clear has been the cause of the climatic changes. Many **CONCEDE** (admit) the existence of the trend but claim that the current trend is merely part of a natural **METEOROLOGICAL** (having to do with weather) cycle. Others lay the blame on humans' emission of greenhouse gases. According to Richard A. Muller, a former **SKEPTIC** (Word 102) whose Berkeley Earth Surface Temperature project has persuaded him of human **CULPABILITY** (blameworthiness) in global warming, the changes are too great to be **ASCRIBED** (attributed) to urban heating, solar activity, world population, normal fluctuations, or manipulation of data. Only changes in the carbon dioxide curve match the changes in world temperatures. So, the **SKEPTIC** has been persuaded that man is, **INCONTROVERTIBLY**, playing a part in the climate changes we are now experiencing.

71 | VORACIOUS, RAVENOUS, RAPACIOUS
Having a huge appetite that cannot be satisfied; INSATIABLE

What do Homer (*The Simpsons*), Bluto (*Animal House*), and Scooby-Doo (*Scooby Do! Mystery Incorporated*) have in common? All three have **VORACIOUS** appetites. Homer has an **INSATIABLE** appetite for frosted doughnuts. Bluto regularly and **RAPACIOUSLY** piles great quantities of food on his plate. Scooby has a **RAVENOUS** appetite for Scooby Snacks, and he habitually sneaks food from the plates of his friends.

72 | CALLOUS
Emotionally hardened; insensitive; unfeeling

In the movie *Mean Girls*, the Plastics **CALLOUSLY** mistreat their classmates. They even keep a "Burn Book" filled with **CALLOUS INNUENDOES** (Word 66) and **SARCASTIC** (Word 3) putdowns.

In F. Scott Fitzgerald's novel *The Great Gatsby*, Tom Buchanan **CALLOUSLY** ruins the lives of four people (Daisy, Gatsby, Myrtle, and George) while recklessly pursuing his own selfish pleasures.

73 | INTREPID, UNDAUNTED
Courageous; RESOLUTE (Word 359); fearless

What do Luke Skywalker and Charles Lindbergh have in common? Both were **INTREPID** pilots who were **UNDAUNTED** by seemingly impossible odds. In the movie *Star Wars: Episode IV*, Luke was **UNDAUNTED** by the Empire's seemingly invincible Death Star. The **INTREPID** Skywalker destroyed the Death Star with well-aimed proton torpedoes.

The American aviator Charles Lindbergh was also **UNDAUNTED** by a seemingly impossible task. Despite several attempts, no pilot had successfully flown across the Atlantic. In 1927, the **INTREPID** Lindbergh electrified the world by flying his single-engine plane, the *Spirit of St. Louis*, from New York to Paris in a grueling 33-hour and 39-minute flight.

74 | NONCHALANT

Having an air of casual indifference; coolly unconcerned; ***UNFLAPPABLE***

When you are driving, do you slow down for a yellow light and promptly stop for a red light? We hope so. While careful and law-abiding drivers follow these rules of the road, not all drivers do. Italian drivers are famous for their **NONCHALANT** attitude toward yellow and even red lights. One typical Italian cab driver **NONCHALANTLY** explained that lights are merely advisory: "Everyone drives through yellow lights and fresh red ones. It is no big deal." Needless to say, we hope you will not take such a **NONCHALANT** attitude.

75 | CONVOLUTED

Winding, twisting, and therefore difficult to understand; intricate

What do the Electoral College and the Bowl Championship Series (BCS) have in common? Both require a **CONVOLUTED** process to choose a winner. The Electoral College requires a **CONVOLUTED** process to choose a President, and the BCS requires a **CONVOLUTED** process to choose two football teams to play for the national championship.

76 | ITINERANT

Migrating from place to place; NOT ***SEDENTARY***

During the Great Awakening, George Whitefield and other **ITINERANT** ministers touring the Colonies preached their message of human helplessness and divine **OMNIPOTENCE** (infinite power). Today, many movie stars also live **ITINERANT** lives. For example, during the last six years, Angelina Jolie and Brad Pitt have lived in 15 homes all over the world, including Paris, Prague, Los Angeles, New Orleans, Berlin, Namibia, India, and New York City. Jolie enjoys her **ITINERANT** lifestyle and says that it is important to experience a variety of cultures.

77 | POIGNANT
Moving; touching; heartrending

In the movie *Remember the Titans*, Gerry Bertier and Julius Campbell are forced to become teammates on the racially-divided T.C. Williams High School football team. Although originally bitter rivals, they overcome their prejudices and become close friends. When Julius visits the paralyzed Gerry in the hospital, the nurse bars Julius, who is black, from the room, saying, "Only kin's allowed in here." But Gerry corrects her: "Alice, are you blind? Don't you see the family resemblance? That's my brother." This **POIGNANT** scene brought tears to the eyes of many viewers.

78 | IMPETUS
A stimulus or encouragement that results in increased activity

Lord Voldemort's resurrection at the end of *Harry Potter and the Goblet of Fire* provided the **IMPETUS** for the revival of the Order of the Phoenix and the formation of Dumbledore's Army.

Although it was a failure, Shays' Rebellion in 1786 alarmed key American colonial leaders, thus providing the **IMPETUS** for calling a convention to revise and strengthen the Articles of Confederation.

79 | BUCOLIC, RUSTIC, PASTORAL
Characteristic of charming, unspoiled countryside and the simple, rural life

Americans have always been proud of our country's great natural beauty. During the early 19th century, a group of artists known as the Hudson River School specialized in painting the **RUSTIC** beauty of America's unspoiled landscape. Today, many students are attracted to the **PASTORAL** beauty of campuses located in small towns. For example, one writer described Blacksburg, Virginia, the home of Virginia Tech, as "a quaint, off-the-beaten-track, **BUCOLIC** college town nestled in the mountains of southwest Virginia."

80 | EQUANIMITY
Calmness; composure; even-temperedness; poise

George Washington, the great Father of America, was known for his **EQUANIMITY**. He maintained composure no matter what happened around him. Faced with the dangers of battle during the Revolutionary War, Washington remained even-tempered and unflappable. His ability to maintain composure in the heat of battle encouraged his troops to follow and respect him, even during the most devastating times in the Revolution. His **EQUANIMITY** made him an indispensable leader in the early years of the fledgling nation.

81 | PANACHE, VERVE, FLAMBOYANCE, ÉLAN (Word 316)
Great vigor and energy; dash, especially in artistic performance and composition

During the Middle Ages, proud European military commanders often placed feathers or a plume in their helmets as they rode into battle. Known as a *panache*, the feathers and plumes helped troops identify their commander but also made him an easier target for enemy arrows and bullets. Given the risk, it took real courage for a commander to wear a *panache*.

Today the word **PANACHE** no longer refers to feathers or a plume. But **PANACHE** still retains its sense of **VERVE** or dash. **PANACHE** is now most frequently used to refer to **FLAMBOYANT** entertainers. For example, Lady Gaga is one of the music world's most **FLAMBOYANT** performers.

82 | PROVOCATIVE
Provoking discussion; stimulating controversy; arousing a reaction

Prior to World War I, young women aspired to seem modest and maidenly. But that changed during the Roaring Twenties. Once **DEMURE** (modest) maidens now **PROVOCATIVELY** proclaimed their new freedom by becoming "flappers." Flappers shocked their elders by dancing the Charleston and wearing one-piece bathing suits. Dismayed by this **PROVOCATIVE** clothing, officials at some beaches insisted on measuring the length of the bathing suits to make sure that they did not reveal too much of the women's legs. In today's world, this notion of **PROVOCATIVE** would seem **ARCHAIC** (Word 25)!

83 | PLACID, SERENE
Calm or quiet; undisturbed by tumult or disorder

What do the Pacific Ocean and the SAT word **PLACID** have in common? When the legendary explorer Ferdinand Magellan left the Strait of Magellan, he entered an immense and as yet unexplored body of water that he described as a *Mare Pacificum* or "peaceful sea."

KNOW YOUR ROOTS		
LATIN ROOT: ***PLAC*** | to quiet, soothe, pacify, please	IMPLACABLE PLACATE PLACID COMPLACENT COMPLAISANT (Word 335)	unappeasable, inexorable to appease or calm someone's anger calm, quiet self-satisfied, smug disposed to please (note French *plaisir*), affable, gracious

84 | FORTUITOUS
Of accidental but fortunate occurrence; having unexpected good fortune

In the fall of 1862, the South appeared to be on the verge of victory in the Civil War. Following a brilliant triumph at the Second Battle of Bull Run, General Robert E. Lee boldly invaded Maryland. In war, however, decisive battles are often determined as much by **FORTUITOUS** accident as by carefully-planned strategy. As Lee's army steadily advanced, a Union corporal discovered a bulky envelope lying in the grass near a shade tree. Curious, he picked it up and discovered three cigars wrapped in a piece of paper containing Lee's secret battle plans. This **FORTUITOUS** discovery played a key role in enabling the Union forces to win a pivotal victory at the Battle of Antietam.

85 | DISPEL

To drive away; scatter, as to DISPEL a misconception

The first administration of the SAT occurred in 1901, and since then quite a few myths have arisen. We're here to **DISPEL** a couple of misconceptions you might have.

Myth: The SAT is a reasoning test; you can't study for it.
Absolutely not! The book you're holding right now, *Direct Hits*, can help you ace the sentence completions and boost your critical reading score.

Myth: It's always better to leave a question blank than to guess on the SAT.
Not necessarily. You receive a full point for correct answers, gain zero points for incorrect answers, and lose a quarter point for incorrect answers. But if you can eliminate one or two incorrect answers in a multiple choice, your odds of answering correctly improve dramatically.

On the sentence completions section, if you see a Direct Hits word in the answer choices, but you're sure it's not the correct answer (an indirect hit), you can eliminate this answer and greatly improve your chances of guessing correctly.

To further **DISPEL** this misconception, remember what Wayne Gretzky says: "You miss 100 percent of the shots you don't take."

86 | AMALGAM

A mixture; a blend; a combination of different elements

Rap star Ludacris' name is actually an **AMALGAM**. He combined his birth name Cris and his radio handle Luda to **COIN** (Word 296) the new name—LUDACRIS!

Similarly, rap star Jay-Z's name is also an **AMALGAM**. Shawn Carter grew up in Brooklyn near where the J-Z subway line has a stop on Marcy Avenue. Carter's friends nicknamed him "Jazzy." Carter later combined the name of the subway line with his nickname to **COIN** the new name Jay-Z!

87 | VIABLE, FEASIBLE
Capable of being accomplished; possible

Soaring oil costs and worries about global warming have prompted a search for **VIABLE** alternatives to fossil fuels. Some of the most **FEASIBLE** alternative energy sources include solar power, wind power, and biofuels. However, currently only around eight percent of energy in the United States comes from renewable sources, meaning that much research is still needed in order to find **VIABLE** alternative energy sources. Companies like BP and GE have invested billions of dollars in research on the most **FEASIBLE** sources of energy.

88 | ANGUISH
Agonizing physical or mental pain; torment

Ancient Greek tragedies are filled with the unhappiness, pain, failure, and loss associated with the human condition. In Sophocles's *Antigone* King Creon of Thebes has refused to give his nephew a proper burial after he was killed in a battle against his own brother. Creon's niece Antigone, **ANGUISHED** at this **BREACH** (break) of protocol, tries to carry out the funeral rites and is **IMMURED** (walled up) in a cave as punishment. Creon remains **OBDURATE** (Word 15) until he hears of the suicides of his wife and his son (Antigone's fiancé) after Antigone hangs herself. Too late **REMORSEFUL** (Word 432), Creon is left to deal with his **ANGUISH** totally alone.

When Bruce Wayne saved Gotham from the Joker in *The Dark Knight*, he sustained multiple injuries, allowed his Batman alter ego to be declared a criminal, and lost the love of his life, Rachel Dawes. Set eight years later, *The Dark Knight Rises* finds Bruce frail, **RECLUSIVE** (Word 113), and filled with **ANGUISH** over Rachel's death. However, Bruce dons the Batman suit again when a **MALEVOLENT** (Word 218) and strong terrorist named Bane threatens Gotham. The brutal Bane proves to be a **BANE** (Word 16) for Batman, who has met his match in the powerful masked villain. Wayne finds himself in physical **ANGUISH** after a devastating encounter with Bane.

89 | INTEMPERATE
Lacking restraint; excessive

TEMPERATE
Exercising moderation and restraint

INTEMPERATE habits such as smoking, drinking, and overeating are **INIMICAL** (harmful) to good health. In contrast, a **TEMPERATE** person leads a lifestyle characterized by moderation and self-restraint. Bluto (*Animal House*), Frank "The Tank" (*Old School*), and Ben Stone (*Knocked Up*) were all fun-loving, **INTEMPERATE** party animals. Compare their lifestyles to Andy Stitzer's (*The 40-Year-Old Virgin*) far more **TEMPERATE** approach to life.

The 18th century British author Samuel Johnson is famed for saying, "**ABSTINENCE** (refraining from use) is as easy to me as **TEMPERANCE** would be difficult."

90 | SUPERFICIAL
Shallow; lacking in depth; concerned with surface appearances

What do Cher (*Clueless*) and Daisy Buchanan (*The Great Gatsby*) have in common? Both are **SUPERFICIAL**. In *Clueless*, Josh calls Cher "a **SUPERFICIAL** space cadet" because she lacks direction. Daisy proves to be a **SUPERFICIAL** person who prizes material possessions. For example, she bursts into tears when Gatsby shows her his collection of English dress shirts because she realizes that he has now become seriously wealthy. Tragically, Gatsby discovers that beneath Daisy's **SUPERFICIAL** surface there is only more surface.

KNOW YOUR ROOTS		
LATIN PREFIX:		
SUPER, *SUPRA*	over, above, greater in quality	SUPERCILIOUS — overbearing, proud, haughty
		SUPERFICIAL — on the surface, shallow
		SUPERLATIVE — the best, in the highest degree
		SUPERNATURAL — above and beyond all nature
		SUPERSEDE — to take the place of, to SUPPLANT

91 | LAUD, EXTOL, TOUT, ACCLAIM
To praise; to applaud

Tip for a Direct Hit

LAUDS is the morning church service in which psalms of praise to God are sung. Note that the word appLAUD contains the root word LAUD. LAUD and its synonyms EXTOL, TOUT, and ACCLAIM all mean to praise.

What do the Beach Boys' classic song "California Girls" and Katy Perry's hit "California Gurls" have in common? Both songs **EXTOL** the beauty of California girls. The Beach Boys acknowledge that they are **BEGUILED** (enticed, captivated) by the way southern girls talk. They **LAUD** east coast girls for being hip. However, this doesn't shake their **CONVICTION** (firm belief) that California girls are "the cutest girls in the world."

Needless to say, Katy Perry **CONCURS** (agrees) with the Beach Boys. She proudly **TOUTS** the beauty of California's **ACCLAIMED** golden coast. But that is not all. The California boys "break their necks" trying to sneak a peek at the **VOLUPTUOUS** (very sensual) "California gurls." And who can blame them? According to Katy, "California gurls" are "unforgettable Daisy Dukes, bikinis on top."

92 | DISMISSIVE
Showing overt intentional INDIFFERENCE (Word 10) or disregard; rejecting

What do the artist Jackson Pollock, the author J.K. Rowling, and the reggae singer and rapper Sean Kingston have in common? All three had to overcome **DISMISSIVE** critics. Bewildered critics ridiculed Pollock, calling him "Jack the Dripper." **INDIFFERENT** (Word 10) editors at numerous publishing houses rejected J.K. Rowling's story about a boy wizard named Harry Potter. And Sean Kingston almost quit the music industry after his idols Timbaland and Pharrell **DISMISSED** his early recordings.

KNOW YOUR ROOTS		
LATIN ROOT:	EMIT	to send out
MITT/MISS | to send	SUBMIT	to send under, yield, resign, surrender
	TRANSMIT	to send across, communicate, convey
	REMIT	to send back, pay money, diminish in intensity
	OMIT	to send by, pass by, neglect, leave out
	ADMIT	to send to, let in, confess, concede
	COMMIT	to send together, entrust, pledge, memorize
	PERMIT	to send through, allow
	DISMISS	to send away, discharge, put out of mind
	REMISS	(adj.) negligent, lax, careless
	REMITTANCE	a payment sent to pay a bill
	MISSION	a duty one is sent to perform
	MISSILE	something sent through the air
	MISSIVE	a note sent by messenger
	EMISSARY	a messenger sent on a mission

93 | DISPARAGE

To speak of in a slighting or disrespectful way; to belittle

Did you see the movie *Transformers: Revenge of the Fallen*? What was your opinion? Does it deserve to be **LAUDED** (Word 91) or **DISPARAGED**? You might be surprised to learn that Megan Fox, the actress who played Mikaela Banes, **DISPARAGED** *Transformers* director Michael Bay for focusing more on special effects than on acting. Fox also blasted Bay, calling him a dictator "who wants to be like Hitler on his sets." **GALLED** (irked) by Fox's **DISPARAGING** remarks, Bay shot back that Fox is young "and has a lot of growing to do." Bay finally ended the war of words when he cut Fox from *Transformers: Dark Of The Moon*, saying her role was not **INTEGRAL** (essential) to the story.

94 | POMPOUS

Filled with excessive self-importance; PRETENTIOUS;
OSTENTATIOUS (Word 413); boastful

In the Harry Potter **SAGA** (Word 236), Draco Malfoy is a bully who arrogantly proclaims that pure-blood wizards are far superior to Muggles (non-wizards) and Mudbloods (Muggle-born witches and wizards). The **POMPOUS** Malfoy loves to use verbal taunts to **DENIGRATE** (malign) Harry, Ron, and Hermione. Draco is a literary **FOIL** (contrast) to the modest hero, Harry Potter.

95 | CRYPTIC

Having a hidden or AMBIGUOUS (Word 21) meaning; mysterious

As *Harry Potter and the Chamber of Secrets* opens, Dobby delivers this **CRYPTIC** message to Harry: "Harry Potter must not go back to Hogwarts." But why must Harry stay away from Hogwarts? Since the message is so **CRYPTIC**, we don't know. Later in the same book, a **CRYPTIC** message appears on one of the walls at Hogwarts: "The Chamber of Secrets has been opened. Enemies of the Heir, Beware." Once again, since the message is **CRYPTIC**, we are not sure what it means.

96 | SUBTLE

Difficult to detect; faint; mysterious; likely to elude perception

Iago, the ultimate villain of English literature, is brilliantly **SUBTLE** in the way he manipulates Othello into believing that his wife, Desdemona, has been unfaithful. Iago **SUBTLY** plants suspicion with diversions, suggestions, and **INNUENDOES** (Word 66). This **SUBTLETY** makes Othello more deeply **APPREHENSIVE** (wary), and so Iago's **NEFARIOUS** (Word 139) plan succeeds in destroying both Othello and Desdemona.

97 | DISPARITY

An inequality; a gap; an imbalance

Tip for a Direct Hit

DISPARITY contains the Latin root *PAR* meaning "that which is equal." The root still lives in the golfing term *PAR*, which means to be equal to the course. It can also be seen in the SAT word PARITY, which means equality in status or value.

The Hunger Games takes place in the nation of Panem, which contains 12 districts controlled by the **DESPOTIC** (Word 270) President Snow, who rules the country from the Capitol. There is great **DISPARITY** in Panem between the **AFFLUENT** (having a great deal of money, wealthy) and spoiled citizens of the Capitol and the **IMPECUNIOUS** (Word 138) residents of the districts, who live in **DEPLORABLE** (very bad) conditions and suffer from starvation. The **DISPARITY** is especially evident during the annual Hunger Games, in which the districts are forced to send teenagers to compete in a **MORTAL** (deadly) battle for the Capitol's entertainment.

Mumbai (formerly Bombay) is India's financial capital and largest city. The movie *Slumdog Millionaire* features vivid images of the **DISPARITY** between the **AFFLUENT** (Word 257) few who live in the city's luxury condominiums and the poverty-stricken masses who live in tiny shacks in the densely-crowded Dharavi slum.

98 | CURTAIL

To cut short or reduce

The 2010 Gulf Oil Spill created an **UNPRECEDENTED** (Word 285) environmental and economic disaster. As a toxic oil slick spread across the Gulf's once **PRISTINE** (Word 417) beaches and wetlands, **IRATE** (angry, incensed) workers lost jobs while worried tourists **CURTAILED** and even canceled vacation trips to the region. The spill **UNDERSCORED** (emphasized) America's dependence upon gasoline. On average, Americans consume about 386 million gallons of gasoline each day. This **PRODIGIOUS** (huge) rate of consumption cannot go on forever. Many **PUNDITS** (Word 117) argue that Americans must **CURTAIL** their fuel consumption by developing renewable sources of energy.

99 | INNOCUOUS

Harmless; unlikely to give offense or to arouse strong feelings or hostility; not INIMICAL

Many mushrooms are **INNOCUOUS**, but there are some, like the Amanita or Death Cap mushroom, that are poisonous and should not be eaten.

Sometimes a person will say something unkind and then claim that the intent was **INNOCUOUS**, saying, "Oh, they know I'm kidding." Such an assertion may very well be **DISINGENUOUS** (Word 428), for the speaker is probably quite aware of the toxic effect of the not-so-**INNOCUOUS** words.

100 | DIATRIBE, TIRADE, HARANGUE

A bitter abusive denunciation; a thunderous verbal attack; a RANT

What do Coach Carter (*Coach Carter*), Coach Gaines (*Friday Night Lights*), and Coach Boone (*Remember the Titans*) all have in common? All three coaches are passionate about building character and team-work. And, if necessary, all three don't hesitate to deliver a **TIRADE** when a player fails to follow team rules or perform to the best of his ability. For example, Coach Boone demands perfection. In one memorable **DIATRIBE** he insists, "We will be perfect in every aspect of the game. You drop a pass, you run a mile. You miss a blocking assignment, you run a mile. You fumble the football, and I will break my foot off in your John Brown hind parts and then you will run a mile. Perfection. Let's go to work!"

It is debatable as to whether **HARANGUING** others in order to inspire them to different behaviours is an effective strategy. Former Indianapolis Colts' coach, Tony Dungy, refused to **RANT** at his players and achieved great success including winning the Superbowl.

CHAPTER 3

You Meet The Most Interesting People On The SAT | 101 – 130

History is filled with a fascinating array of men and women who have made enduring contributions or caused great tragedies. This chapter will introduce you to 30 SAT words that describe an astonishing variety of people. You will meet Pharaoh Akhenaton, the ancient world's most famous **ICONOCLAST** (Word 107), and William Lloyd Garrison, the **ZEALOT** (Word 118), who championed the cause of the unconditional and immediate abolition of slavery. As you study this chapter, you will learn words that will help you describe great orators, notorious traitors, and astute political commentators. We are convinced that you meet the most interesting people on the SAT!

101 | CHARLATAN

A fake; fraud; imposter; cheat

<table>
<tr><td>

Tip for a Direct Hit

The word CHARLATAN often appears in sentence completion questions. A CHARLATAN is associated with negative traits. A CHARLATAN will try to DUPE (mislead) UNWARY (incautious) victims with SPURIOUS (false) information.

</td><td>

Would you trust the Wizard of Oz, Gilderoy Lockhart (*Harry Potter and the Chamber of Secrets*), or Chaucer's Friar (*The Canterbury Tales*)? I hope not. All three of these men were **CHARLATANS**, imposters who could not be trusted. The Wizard of Oz was a **CHARLATAN** who tried to trick Dorothy and her friends. Gilderoy Lockhart was a **CHARLATAN** who interviewed famous wizards and witches and then took credit for their heroic deeds. The Friar, a member of a medieval **MENDICANT** (begging) order, was supposed to beg from the rich and give to the poor. Instead, he spent his time with well-off people, knew all the taverns,

</td></tr>
</table>

and dispensed pardons based solely on the amount of money he was given. It is even suggested that he had an active love life that required him to find husbands for the young women he had made pregnant.

102 | SKEPTIC

A person who doubts, asks questions, and lacks faith

In the movie *Men in Black*, Edwards was originally a **SKEPTIC** who did not believe that aliens were actually living in New York City. In *Bruce Almighty*, Bruce was originally a **SKEPTIC** who did not believe that the man he met was really God. And in the movie *Superbad*, Seth was originally a **SKEPTIC** who did not believe that Fogell's fake Hawaiian ID, with the name "McLovin", would work.

103 | RHETORICIAN

An eloquent writer or speaker; a master of RHETORIC (the art of speaking and writing)

Frederick Douglass, Franklin Roosevelt, Martin Luther King Jr., John F. Kennedy, and Ronald Reagan were all **CHARISMATIC** (magnetic and inspiring) leaders and superb **RHETORICIANS**, whose eloquent speeches inspired millions of people. For example, in his inaugural address, President Kennedy challenged Americans by proclaiming, "And so, my fellow Americans: ask not what your country can do for you—ask what you can do for your country."

104 | HEDONIST

A person who believes that pleasure is the chief goal of life

In Ancient Greece, the **HEDONISTS** urged their followers to "eat, drink, and be merry, for tomorrow we die." Although it is a long way from Ancient Greece to the home of rapper Ricky Ross in Miami, the **HEDONISTIC** principle of pursuing pleasure remains the same. During the tour of his "crib," Ross proudly displays the interior of his Escalade Maybach, a Cadillac Escalade with the interior of a Maybach. Hooked up with leather seats, plasmas, and satellites, the interior provides everything a **HEDONIST** could possibly ask for.

105 | ASCETIC

A person who gives up material comforts and leads a life of self-denial, especially as an act of religious devotion

At the age of 29, Prince Siddhartha Gautama left the luxuries of his father's palace and for the next six years adopted an extreme **ASCETIC** life. For days at a time, he ate only a single grain of rice. His stomach became so empty that, by poking a finger into it, he could touch his backbone. Yet, Gautama found only pain, not wisdom. He decided to give up extreme **ASCETICISM** and seek wisdom in other ways. Gautama was successful and soon became known as Buddha, a title meaning "the Enlightened One."

106 | RACONTEUR

A person who excels in telling ANECDOTES

Herodotus was an ancient Greek historian who was a renowned **RACONTEUR**. Many of the **ANECDOTES** (Word 238) in the movie *300* are taken from his famous history of the Persian Wars. For example, Herodotus recounts how a Persian officer tried to intimidate the Spartans by declaring, "A thousand nations of the Persian Empire descend upon you. Our arrows will blot out the sun." **UNDAUNTED** (Word 73), the Spartan warrior Stelios retorted, "Then we will fight in the shade."

107 | ICONOCLAST

A person who attacks and ridicules cherished figures, ideas, and institutions

What do the Egyptian pharaoh Akhenaton and the modern filmmaker Michael Moore have in common? Both are **ICONOCLASTS**. Akhenaton challenged ancient Egypt's longstanding belief in a large number of gods by rejecting polytheism and insisting that Aton was the universal or only god. Michael Moore is a modern **ICONOCLAST** whose documentary films have attacked the Iraq War, the American health care system, Wall Street bankers, and Washington politicians. Like a true **ICONOCLAST**, Moore ridiculed Congress, saying that most of its members are scoundrels who deserve to be "removed and replaced."

108 | PARTISAN

A supporter of a person, party, or cause; a person with strong and perhaps biased beliefs

Are you pro-life or pro-choice? Do you support health care reform legislation? How do you feel about illegal immigration? If you have a strong view on these issues, you are a **PARTISAN**. In contrast, **NONPARTISAN** issues enjoy widespread public support. For example, during the Cold War, most Americans supported the policy of containing Soviet expansion.

109 | POLYMATH

A person whose expertise spans a significant number of subject areas

DILETTANTE

An amateur or dabbler; a person with a SUPERFICIAL (Word 90) interest in an art or a branch of knowledge; a trifler

Tip for a Direct Hit

DILETTANTE comes from the Italian, meaning a "lover of the arts" and goes back to the Latin *dilettare*, to delight.

Originally it did not carry the PEJORATIVE (negative) connotations that it holds today. In the 17th and 18th centuries, people were more inclined to celebrate the "well-rounded Renaissance man." Perhaps it was easier to master a number of fields when there was less to be known.

POLYMATH Benjamin Franklin (1706-1790), noted author, printer, inventor, scientist, political theorist, musician, satirist, diplomat, and statesman, had a **MYRIAD** (Word 352) of interests, all of which he developed to a remarkable degree. His diligence, intelligence, common sense, strength of character, and **TENACITY** (Word 56) helped him to become one of the most influential of the Founding Fathers.

In contrast, Max Fischer, a high school sophomore in Wes Anderson's movie *Rushmore*, is flunking every subject, but he is involved in virtually every extra-curricular activity offered at his school. The **BIZARRE** (conspicuously unusual) list of activities—from Beekeeping to Debate to JV Decathlon to Second Chorale Director—**SATIRIZES** (Word 233) the culture of the **DILETTANTE**, a "Jack of all trades, but master of none."

In recent years colleges have been sending the message that they would prefer candidates who **DELVE** (dig) deeply into one or several areas of interest instead of those who pad their resumés with long lists of activities that could only have commanded **DILETTANTISH** attention.

110 | MENTOR

An advisor; a teacher; a guide

ACOLYTE

A devoted follower

In the *Star Wars* **SAGA** (Word 236), Obi-Wan Kenobi is a Jedi Knight who serves as Luke Skywalker's **MENTOR**. As an eager young **ACOLYTE** of the **SAGE** (profoundly wise) Kenobi, Skywalker learns the ways of the Force, a natural power harnessed by the Jedi in their struggle against the **VILLAINOUS** (vile, **DEPRAVED**, wicked) Darth Vader and the evil Galactic Empire.

111 | DEMAGOGUE

A leader who appeals to the fears, emotions, and prejudices of the populace

Adolf Hitler is often cited as the **EPITOME** (perfect example) of a **DEMAGOGUE**. Hitler rose to power by using impassioned speeches that appealed to the ethnic and nationalistic prejudices of the German people. Hitler exploited, embittered, and misled WWI veterans by blaming their plight on minorities and other convenient scapegoats.

Unfortunately, Americans have not been immune to the impassioned pleas of **DEMAGOGUES**. During the 1950s Senator Joseph McCarthy falsely alleged that Communist sympathizers had infiltrated the State Department. As McCarthy's **DEMAGOGIC** rhetoric grew bolder, he **DENOUNCED** (Word 177) General George Marshall, former Army Chief of Staff and ex-Secretary of State, calling him "part of a conspiracy so immense and an infamy so black as to dwarf any previous venture in the history of man."

112 | AUTOMATON

A self-operating machine; a mindless follower; a person who acts in a mechanical fashion

In the Harry Potter series, the Imperius Curse was a spell that caused its victim to fall under the command of the caster. In *Harry Potter and the Deathly Hallows*, the Death Eater Yaxley placed an Imperius Curse on Pius Thickness. When Thickness became Minister of Magic, he behaved like an **AUTOMATON** or mindless follower of Lord Voldemort.

113 | RECLUSE

A person who leads a secluded or solitary life

In *The 40-Year-Old Virgin*, Andy Stitzer was a complete **RECLUSE** until he started hanging out with his coworkers from SmartTech. Andy's only hobbies were collecting action figures, playing video games, and watching *Survivor*. In fact, Andy was so **RECLUSIVE** that when a coworker asked him what the highlight of his weekend was, Andy recounted the adventures of making an egg salad sandwich!

Another example of a **RECLUSE** is Harper Lee. Although she is the world-famous Pulitzer Prize-winning author of *To Kill A Mockingbird*, she rarely ever appears in public.

114 | BUNGLER

Someone who is clumsy or INEPT; a person who makes mistakes because of incompetence

BUNGLERS have been featured in a number of movies. For example, in the movie *21 Jump Street*, officers Morton Schmidt and Greg Jenko are **BUNGLERS** who botch their investigations and police work. They forget to read the *Miranda* rights to a criminal during an arrest, confuse their undercover identities, and even get fired from the Jump Street division for their **INEPT** work.

In the movie *The Princess Diaries*, Mia Thermopolis is a **BUNGLER** who is **INEPT** in social situations, awkward and clumsy. However, she discovers that she's the princess of Genovia, a small European country. After taking many "Princess Lessons," she emerges as a confident princess, fit to rule her country.

115 | CLAIRVOYANT

Having the supposed power to see objects and events that cannot be perceived with the five traditional senses; as a noun, a SEER

Sybill Trelawney was the Divination professor at Hogwarts who claimed to be a **CLAIRVOYANT**. She used tea leaves and crystal balls to see the future. Both Harry and Professor Dumbledore were **SKEPTICAL** (Word 102) about her claim to be a **CLAIRVOYANT**. In *Harry Potter and the Order of the Phoenix*, Dolores Umbridge fired Sybill for being a **CHARLATAN** (Word 101). Nonetheless, readers of the Harry Potter series know that Trelawney did make two extremely important and very accurate prophecies.

In the show *Psych*, Shawn Spencer convinces the police department that he is **CLAIRVOYANT**, and they hire him as a psychic consultant. However, he is a **CHARLATAN** (Word 101), for he is not actually **CLAIRVOYANT**. Instead, he is extremely observant and has a keen memory. His exceptional observational and **DEDUCTIVE** (drawing conclusions based on reasoning from the general to the particular) skills allow him to maintain his charade as a psychic since they help him solve complex cases.

116 | PROGNOSTICATOR

A person who makes predictions based upon current information and data

Weather forecasters, sports announcers, and financial analysts are all **PROGNOSTICATORS** who use information and data to make predictions and forecasts. It is important to understand the difference between a **PROGNOSTICATOR** and a **CLAIRVOYANT** (Word 115).

Although both make predictions, a **PROGNOSTICATOR** uses empirical data that can be collected, seen, and studied. In contrast, a **CLAIRVOYANT** claims to see the future through means beyond the five senses.

In medicine, a doctor will often give a patient his **PROGNOSIS** (a forecast concerning the causes of his disease and outlining the chances of recovery).

117 | PUNDIT

An expert commentator; an authority who expresses his or her opinion, usually on political issues

From CNN's News Center to ESPN's Sports Center, television programs are filled with **PUNDITS** who offer their "expert" commentary on issues ranging from political campaigns to March Madness brackets. The **PUNDITS** almost always sound authoritative and convincing. But it is wise to maintain a healthy **SKEPTICISM** (Word 102). Here are expert opinions from famous pundits who turned out to be wrong:

"Louis Pasteur's theory of germs is ridiculous fiction."
Pierre Packet, Professor of Physiology at Toulouse, 1872

"Heavier-than-air flying machines are impossible."
Lord Kelvin, President of the Royal Society, 1895

"Stocks have reached what looks like a permanently high plateau."
Irving Fisher, Professor of Economics, Yale University, 1929

"There is no reason anyone would want a computer in their home."
Ken Olson, President, Chairman, and Founder of Digital Equipment Corp., 1977

118 | ZEALOT

A very enthusiastic person; a champion; a true believer, perhaps to an excessive degree; a fanatic

William Lloyd Garrison was a **ZEALOT** who championed the cause of unconditional and immediate abolition of slavery. In the first issue of *The Liberator*, Garrison left no doubt as to his intentions when he wrote: "I am in earnest—I will not **EQUIVOCATE** (Word 215)—I will not excuse—I will not retreat a single inch—AND I WILL BE HEARD."

119 | NEOPHYTE, NOVICE, GREENHORN
A beginner; someone new to a field or activity

In October 2008 Justin Bieber was an unknown **NEOPHYTE** who had never professionally recorded a song. However, Usher recognized that although Bieber was a **NOVICE**, he was a musical **PRODIGY** (Word 123) with the potential to become a superstar. With Usher as his **MENTOR** (Word 110), Bieber quickly **MORPHED** (transformed) from a **GREENHORN** into a global sensation. No longer a **NOVICE**, Bieber has begun **MENTORING** and promoting other musical **GREENHORNS**. After hearing Carly Rae Jepsen's song "Call Me Maybe," he tweeted about the song and convinced his manager to sign the Canadian singer. "Call Me Maybe" became the source of numerous **PARODIES** (Word 233) that were very popular and became a major hit.

120 | BENEFACTOR, PATRON
A person who makes a gift or bequest
BENEFICIARY
The recipient of funds, titles, property, and other benefits

Nicholas Sparks has achieved international fame by writing romance novels such as *The Notebook* and *A Walk to Remember* that are often set in New Bern, North Carolina. Residents of New Bern also know Sparks as a generous **BENEFACTOR** and **PATRON** who has donated nearly $1 million to build a state-of-the-art track and field facility for New Bern High School. As the **BENEFICIARIES** of this **MUNIFICENCE** (Word 258), the New Bern Bears have become one of North Carolina's top track and field teams. Note that both **BENEFACTOR** and

BENEFICIARY begin with the Latin root *bene*, which means "good." So a **BENEFACTOR**, like Nicholas Sparks, gives good gifts, and a **BENEFICIARY**, like New Bern High School, receives good gifts.

KNOW YOUR ROOTS		
LATIN ROOT: **BENE** | good, well	BENEFIT	to do good, (noun) a good thing
	BENEFICIAL	good, wholesome
	BENEFICENT	doing good
	BENEFACTOR	one who helps another
	BENEVOLENCE	good will towards others
	BENEDICTION	the act of blessing

121 | DISSEMBLER, PREVARICATOR
A liar and deceiver

In *Mean Girls*, Regina George is a cunning **DISSEMBLER** who deliberately lies to her friends and to her enemies. In the movie *Pirates of the Caribbean: Curse of the Black Pearl*, Captain Barbossa is a **PREVARICATOR** who repeatedly lies to Jack Sparrow, Elizabeth Swann, and Will Turner.

122 | PROPONENT
*One who argues in support of something; an **ADVOCATE**; a champion of a cause*

Although America has faced a number of challenging social problems, our nation has always produced leaders who were strong **PROPONENTS** of reform. For example, during the 19th century, Jane Addams was an outspoken **PROPONENT** of urban settlement houses. Today, former Vice-President Al Gore is a vigorous **ADVOCATE** of implementing measures that will reduce global warming. One way to remember **PROPONENT** is to note that the prefix *pro* means to be *for* something.

KNOW YOUR ROOTS

LATIN ROOT:			
PONE, POSE	to place, set, put	EXPOSE	to set forth, to show for all to see
		DEPOSE	to remove from office
		REPOSE	to rest
		IMPOSE	to place on, as a penalty
		SUPPOSE	to assume to be true
		PROPOSE	to offer, to put forward
		EXPONENT	a person who sets forth or interprets
		POSTPONE	to place later, to delay
		POSIT	to assert, to declare
		POSTURE	(vb) to pose, to assume a fake position
			(n.) placement of the limbs, carriage

123 | PRODIGY

A person with great talent; a young genius

What do Wolfgang Mozart and Pablo Picasso have in common? They were **PRODIGIES** who demonstrated uncanny artistic talent at a young age. Mozart was a child **PRODIGY** who wrote his first symphony at the age of eight and grew into a **PROLIFIC** (Word 381) adult who wrote over 600 pieces of music before his death at the age of 35. Like Mozart, Picasso also demonstrated **PRECOCIOUS** (very advanced) talent, drawing pictures before he could talk. Picasso mastered many styles but is best known as the **PROGENITOR** (originator) of Cubism.

124 | ORACLE

A person considered to be ORACULAR, a source of wise counsel or prophetic opinions

Would you like to know what is going to happen in the future? All you have to do is ask an **ORACLE**. Just as the ancient Greeks asked the Delphic Oracle to predict the future, 2010 World Cup soccer fans watched televised reports featuring the predictions of an octopus named Paul. The eight-legged **ORACLE** became a global sensation when he correctly predicted the winner of eight straight matches.

Paul's **PROGNOSTICATIONS** (Word 116) attracted **LUCRATIVE** (Word 253) offers from people who wanted to know the outcome of elections and the gender of future children.

125 | MISANTHROPE

A person who hates or distrusts humankind

Tip for a Direct Hit

MISANTHROPE combines the Greek prefix *MISO* meaning "hate" with the Greek root *ANTHROPOS* meaning "humankind." Prefixes make a difference in the meaning of words. If we place the Greek prefix *PHILO*, meaning "love," in front of *ANTHROPOS*, we form the word PHILANTHROPY, meaning love of humankind. A PHILANTHROPIST loves humanity so much that he or she donates time and money to charity.

Ebenezer Scrooge and Alceste are two of the best-known **MISANTHROPES** in literature. Scrooge is the main character in Charles Dickens's 1843 novel, *A Christmas Carol*. He is a cold-hearted, **MISERLY** (very stingy) **MISANTHROPE** who despises poor people and Christmas.

Alceste is the main character in Molière's 1666 play, *The Misanthrope*. He is a judgmental **MISANTHROPE**, quick to criticize the flaws in people.

126 | INNOVATOR

A person who introduces something new

Google has now become a verb, synonymous with "to search." But Google was not the first to invent the search engine; others **ANTEDATED** (preceded in time) Google. However, what made Google **INNOVATIVE** was the PageRank algorithm, which ranks websites on their relevance to a search in order to provide the most useful results. Sergey Brin and Larry Page, the **INNOVATORS** behind Google and PageRank, implemented this algorithm, and the rest is history.

INNOVATE incorporates the Latin root *NOV*, meaning "new." For another use of *NOV*, see Word 170.

127 | SYCOPHANT

*A person who seeks favor by flattering people of influence; a **TOADY**; someone who behaves in an **OBSEQUIOUS** (Word 371) or **SERVILE** manner*

Louis XIV compelled France's great nobles to live at the Versailles Palace. Life at the royal palace transformed **HAUGHTY** (arrogant) aristocrats into favor-seeking **SYCOPHANTS**. Instead of competing for political power, nobles **SQUANDERED** (wasted) their fortunes jockeying for social prestige. For example, nobles vied for the **COVETED** (Word 32) honor of holding Louis XIV's shirt as he prepared to get dressed.

128 | STOIC, STOLID

*Seemingly **INDIFFERENT** (Word 10) to or unaffected by joy, grief, pleasure, or pain; impassive and emotionless*

What would you do if you scored the winning goal in a championship soccer game? What would you do if your error caused your team to lose a championship baseball game? Most people would be elated to win and dejected to lose. However, a **STOIC** would remain impassive, showing no emotion in victory or defeat.

Being **STOLID** is not easy. It requires great discipline and self-control. For example, tourists to London are familiar with the distinctive bearskin helmets and scarlet uniforms worn by the guards at Buckingham Palace. The guards are famous for their ability to endure hot summer weather while **STOLIDLY** standing in the same position for hours.

129 | REPROBATE

A morally unprincipled person

Who is the most despised **REPROBATE** living in America today? For thousands of betrayed investors there is only one answer—Bernard

Madoff. On June 29, 2009, Judge Denny Chin sentenced Madoff to 150 years in prison for running a giant Ponzi scheme that cheated investors out of almost $65 billion. Madoff's victims included pension funds, charitable institutions, and elderly retirees. Although Madoff was a **CHARLATAN** (Word 101), he is best described as a **REPROBATE** because of the **ENORMITY** (outrageousness) of a fraud that Judge Chin called "extraordinarily evil."

130 | RENEGADE

A disloyal person who betrays his or her cause; a traitor; a deserter

Tip for a Direct Hit

The words REPROBATE (Word 129) and RENEGADE (Word 130) are easy to confuse. They sound similar, and both are negative words that describe despicable people. A REPROBATE is best remembered as a morally unprincipled and evil person. A RENEGADE is best remembered as a traitor and deserter.

In 1777 Benedict Arnold was one of America's most admired Revolutionary War generals. Yet, just three years later, Arnold was **VILIFIED** (slandered, defamed) as a **RENEGADE** whose name became synonymous with traitor. What happened to cause this amazing change in Arnold's reputation? Despite his bravery at the pivotal battle of Saratoga, Arnold was passed over for promotion while other officers took credit for his accomplishments. Frustrated and bitter, Arnold secretly became a British agent. In 1780, he obtained command of West Point, with plans to surrender it to the British. American forces discovered Arnold's treacherous scheme, and he was forced to flee to London to avoid capture.

Today, Arnold's contributions to the colonial cause are forgotten, and he is remembered as our nation's first and foremost **RENEGADE**.

CHAPTER 4

Every SAT Word Has A History
131 – 155

In 1922 British archaeologist Howard Carter amazed the world by discovering Pharaoh Tutankhamen's tomb. Each of the dazzling artifacts that he unearthed yielded new insights into Egyptian history.

Although we usually don't think of them in this way, words are like historic artifacts. Like the precious jewels Carter found, words also have fascinating histories. **ETYMOLOGY** is a branch of linguistics that specializes in digging up the origins of words.

Each word in our language has a unique history. The English language contains an especially rich collection of words derived from legends, places, customs, and names. These "history-based" words are frequently tested on the SAT.

131 | DRACONIAN
Characterized by very strict laws, rules, and punishments

Draco was an ancient Athenian ruler who believed that the city-state's haphazard judicial system needed to be reformed. In 621 B.C.E., he issued a comprehensive but very severe new code of laws. Whether trivial or serious, most criminal offenses called for the death penalty. Draco's laws were so severe that they were said to be written not in ink but in blood.

Today, the word **DRACONIAN** refers to very strict laws, rules, and punishments. For example, in Iran both men and women can be stoned to death as punishment for being convicted of adultery.

132 | LACONIC
Very brief; concise; SUCCINCT; TERSE

The ancient city-state of Sparta was located in a region of Greece called Laconia. The Spartans were fearless warriors who had little time for long speeches. As a result, they were renowned for being **LACONIC** or very concise. For example, Philip of Macedon, father of Alexander the Great, sent the Spartans a long list of demands. The **LACONIC** Spartans sent it back with a one-word answer: "No!"

Today, the word **LACONIC** still means very brief and **TERSE**.

New Englanders are often described as **LACONIC**. For instance, Robert Frost, the poet who spent most of his life in Vermont and New Hampshire, is considered the **QUINTESSENTIAL** (the most perfect embodiment) **LACONIC** writer, one who expressed much in few words.

133 | SPARTAN
Plain; simple; AUSTERE (Word 19)

The Spartans were more than just **LACONIC**. They also prided themselves on being tough warriors who avoided luxuries and led hardy lives. For example, Spartan soldiers lived in army barracks and ate meager servings of a coarse black porridge.

Today, the word **SPARTAN** still describes a plain life without luxuries. Like the ancient Spartans, American soldiers undergo a rigorous period of training. For example, recruits at the Marine training center at Parris Island must live in **SPARTAN** barracks and endure an **ARDUOUS** (demanding) 12-week training schedule before they can be called United States Marines.

134 | HALCYON

Idyllically calm and peaceful; an untroubled golden time of satisfaction, happiness, and tranquility

In Greek mythology, Alcyone was the daughter of Aeolus, god of the winds, and the devoted wife of Ceyx. When Ceyx tragically drowned in a shipwreck, the distraught Alcyone threw herself into the sea. Out of compassion, the gods transformed Alcyone and Ceyx into a pair of kingfishers. The ancient Greeks named this distinctive bird *halkyon* after Alcyone. According to legend, kingfishers built a floating nest on the sea at about the time of the winter solstice in December. To protect their nest, the gods ordered the winds to remain calm for a week before and after the winter solstice. The expression "halcyon days" refers to this period of untroubled peace and tranquility.

Today, **HALCYON** still refers to a golden time of untroubled happiness and tranquility. In the movie, *The Notebook*, Allie and Noah are two carefree teenagers who meet at a local carnival on Seabrook Island, South Carolina, and spend a romantic summer together. These **HALCYON** days inspire their lifelong love for each other.

Companies can also enjoy **HALCYON** days with content employees, satisfied customers, and robust profits.

135 | SOPHISTRY

A plausible but deliberately misleading or FALLACIOUS argument designed to deceive someone

The Sophists were originally a respected group of ancient Greek philosophers who specialized in teaching rhetoric. However, over time they gained a reputation for their ability to persuade by using clever and often tricky arguments. Today, **SOPHISTRY** is a negative word that refers to a **PLAUSIBLE** (Word 38) but deliberately misleading argument.

In the movie *Animal House*, the Deltas are a notorious group of fun-loving misfits who gleefully break campus rules. Outraged by their low grades and wild parties, Dean Wormer holds a hearing to revoke the Deltas' charter. **UNDAUNTED** (Word 73) by Dean Wormer's accusations, Otter resorts to **SOPHISTRY** in a clever but ultimately **FUTILE** (Word 46) attempt to save the Deltas:

❝*Ladies and gentlemen, I'll be brief. The issue here is not whether we broke a few rules or took a few liberties with our female party guests— we did. But you can't hold a whole fraternity responsible for the behavior of few sick, twisted individuals. For if you do, then shouldn't we blame the whole fraternity system? And if the whole fraternity system is guilty, then isn't this an indictment of our educational institutions in general? I put it to you—isn't this an indictment of our entire American society? Well, you can do whatever you want to us, but we're not going to sit here and listen to you badmouth the United States of America. Gentlemen!*❞

Pleased with his **SOPHISTRY**, Otter then leads the defiant Deltas out of the chamber as all the fraternity brothers hum the Star-Spangled Banner.

136 | CHIMERICAL

Given to fantastic schemes; existing only in the imagination; impossible; vainly conceived

Tip for a Direct Hit

CHIMERICAL is a difficult word that often appears in challenging sentence completion questions. Typically, test writers associate CHIMERICAL with once-promising medical advances that were never fully realized and were thus CHIMERICAL.

The *Chimera* was one of the most fearsome monsters in Greek mythology. A fire-breathing female, she had the head and body of a lion, a serpent's tail, and a goat's head protruding from her midsection. This frightening combination was unusually fantastic even for the ancient Greeks.

Today, a **CHIMERICAL** scheme or claim is one that is a product of unrestrained fantasy. For example, according to popular legend, Ponce de Leon discovered Florida while searching for the fabled Fountain of Youth. While the Fountain of Youth proved to be fanciful, we have still not given up our search for longevity. Fad diets, vitamin supplements, and exercise routines all offer claims that have often proved to be **CHIMERICAL**.

137 | OSTRACIZE

To deliberately exclude from a group; to BANISH

In ancient Athens, an *ostrakon* was a tile or shell. The Athenians used these shells as ballots in an annual vote to decide who, if anyone, should be banished from their city. Each voter wrote a name on his *ostrakon*. If at least 6,000 votes were cast and if a majority of them named one man, then that man was banished or **OSTRACIZED** and had to leave Athens for 10 years because he was thought to be dangerous by the state.

Today, the word **OSTRACIZE** still retains its original meaning of deliberately excluding someone from a group. For example, following World War II, angry French citizens **OSTRACIZED** people who had collaborated with the Nazis. In Chartres, vigilantes shaved the head of a young woman whose baby was fathered by a German soldier. Crowds of jeering people taunted the **OSTRACIZED** woman as she walked alone on the city streets.

138 | IMPECUNIOUS
Poor; penniless; NOT AFFLUENT (Word 257)

When the Romans first settled the lands along the Tiber River, they lacked a metal currency. Nonetheless, Roman farmers did have an ample supply of cattle. As a result, cattle were often used as a measure of wealth. In Latin, *pecus* is the word for cattle. A Roman without a cow or *pecus* was thus **IMPECUNIOUS** (IM is a prefix meaning NOT, see p. 96) or NOT WEALTHY.

Today, the word **IMPECUNIOUS** means lacking money and, thus, poor. The recent global financial crisis is considered by many to be the worst since the Great Depression. The United States' weak economy has **RENDERED** (made) many citizens **IMPECUNIOUS**. The official unemployment rate in the United States reached a staggering 9.1 percent, a figure that did not even include the underemployed or those who had given up looking for work. Moreover, foreclosure rates were at an all-time high, leaving many Americans in a **PRECARIOUS** (Word 205) state financially.

139 | NEFARIOUS
Famous for being wicked; VILLAINOUS; vile

In ancient Rome, the Latin word *nefarius* referred to a criminal. This unsavory connotation continued over the centuries. Today, the word **NEFARIOUS** is used to describe someone who is extremely wicked. Some of the most **NEFARIOUS** villains in film include Lord Voldemort (*Harry Potter*), the Joker (*The Dark Knight*), Darth Vader (*Star Wars*), and the Wicked Witch of the West (*The Wizard of Oz*).

140 | JOVIAL

Good-humored; cheerful; JOCULAR

Jupiter was the chief deity of the Roman **PANTHEON** (all the gods of a particular mythology). The Romans believed that each of their gods possessed particular attributes of character. As the most powerful god, Jupiter was majestic and authoritative. However, he was also believed to be fun-loving and the source of joy and happiness. Since Jupiter was also known as Jove, the word **JOVIAL** came to refer to people who have a cheerful, jolly temperament.

Today, **JOVIAL** still retains its meaning of good-humored, cheerful, and **JOCULAR**. While most people do not associate **JOVIAL** with Jupiter, they do associate the word with Santa Claus. Often referred to as "**JOVIAL** old St. Nicholas," Santa Claus is usually presented as a jolly, good-humored man who brings presents to well-behaved children.

141 | DIRGE

A funeral hymn; a slow, mournful, LUGUBRIOUS (Word 411) musical composition

When medieval Christians gathered to pay their final respects to the deceased, the Church ceremony began with this solemn Latin phrase:

"Dirige, Domine, Deus meus, in conspectu tuo viam meam."
("Direct, O Lord my God, my way in thy sight.")

Today, a **DIRGE** refers to a sad, mournful song or hymn of lament. For example, as the Titanic slowly sank, its musicians supposedly played the **DIRGE** "Nearer, My God, To Thee" to comfort the desperate souls still on the doomed ship. As **POIGNANTLY** (Word 77) depicted in the movie, the band played the **LUGUBRIOUS DIRGE** until the very end. They then calmly went down with their ship.

142 | MAUDLIN

Tearful; excessively sentimental, but not MAWKISH

Mary Magdalene played an important and recurring role in the Gospel accounts of Christ's life and death. According to the Gospels, she stood at the foot of the cross, saw Christ laid in the tomb, and was the first recorded witness of the Resurrection. During the 15th century, artists frequently portrayed Mary Magdalene weeping as Christ was being taken down from the Cross. The word **MAUDLIN** is an alteration of the name Magdalene. Today **MAUDLIN** refers to excessively sentimental behavior.

Fans of the Harry Potter novels will recall that Moaning Myrtle lives up to her name by crying **INCESSANTLY** (endlessly) and thus being **MAUDLIN**. Still, most would agree that she is a strong character who stops short of becoming **MAWKISH** (nauseatingly sentimental in a sickly, dull, **INSIPID** (Word 36) way), which is **MAUDLIN** carried to the extreme.

143 | QUIXOTIC

Foolishly impractical in the pursuit of ideals; impractical idealism

Miguel de Cervantes' epic novel *Don Quixote* describes the chivalric adventures of the would-be knight Don Quixote. Motivated by chivalric ideals, Don Quixote is determined to undo the wrongs of the world. His fertile imagination turns lonely inns into castles and windmills into fearsome giants. After a long series of misadventures, Don Quixote returns home a tired and disillusioned old man. Derived from his name, the modern word **QUIXOTIC** refers to the foolish and impractical pursuit of noble but unattainable ideals.

Every year, 10's of thousands of wannabe singers audition to compete on *American Idol*. Many of the auditionees have left their jobs, skipped important events, and traveled across the country just to attend the auditions. All of the auditionees are convinced that they have the talent to be the next American Idol. The majority of the singers are **QUIXOTIC**, for they give up their livelihoods in order to pursue unrealistic dreams of fame and fortune. Since only a few *Idol* hopefuls make it to the next round, most of the singers return home sadly, with no ticket to Hollywood.

144 | PANDEMONIUM

A wild uproar; tumult

Tip for a Direct Hit

The prefix *PAN* is in a number of words that are ALL around you. For example, a PANORAMIC view enables you to see in ALL directions. A PANACEA is a remedy that will supposedly cure ALL diseases. A PANOPLY is a complete suit of armor and thus any covering that has ALL the necessary array of materials.

In Book I of Milton's *Paradise Lost*, the fallen Satan commands his heralds to announce: "A solemn Councel forthwith to be held/At Pandemonium, the high Capital/of Satan and his Peers." Milton **COINED** (Word 296) this name for the capital of Hell by combining the prefix *PAN*, meaning "all," with the Late Latin word *daemonium*, meaning "place of the evil spirits." As Satan's capital, Pandemonium was characterized by a place of noise, confusion, and wild uproar.

Today, the word **PANDEMONIUM** refers to a wild uproar rather than a specific place. On September 11, 2001, the terrorist attacks on the World Trade Center and the Pentagon created states of **PANDEMONIUM** in New York City and Washington, DC. Recent natural disasters have also caused significant **PANDEMONIUM**. The devastating earthquake in Haiti in January 2010 and the destructive tsunami in Japan in March 2011 caused massive uproar and panic in those countries.

145 | MARTINET

A strict disciplinarian; a person who demands absolute adherence to forms and rules

The French king Louis XIV dreamed of winning glory by expanding France's boundaries to the Rhine River and the Alps. To achieve this goal, Louis and his war minister, the Marquis de Louvois, created Europe's first professional army. In order to be effective, the new army required strict discipline. Louvois assigned this exacting task to

Colonel Jean Martinet. A stern drillmaster, Martinet trained his troops to march in linear formations at exactly 80 paces a minute. The rigid control imposed by Martinet helped transform **NOVICE** (Word 119) soldiers into highly-disciplined fighting units.

Today, the word **MARTINET** still refers to a strict disciplinarian. The Marine Drill Sergeants at Parris Island are renowned for being merciless **MARTINETS**. As readers of Harry Potter are well aware, **MARTINETS** are not limited to the military. In *Harry Potter and the Order of the Phoenix*, Dolores Umbridge was a **MARTINET** who tried to impose rigid standards of discipline on the students and faculty at Hogwarts.

146 | FIASCO
A complete failure; a DEBACLE

Venetian glassblowers were renowned for their skill in making intricate glass vases and bowls. Italian etymologists explain that when a master craftsman discovered a flaw in a piece he was working on, he would turn it into an ordinary bottle to avoid wasting the glass. Since *"far fiasco"* is an Italian phrase meaning "to make a bottle," the bottle would represent a failure and thus a **FIASCO**.

Today, the word **FIASCO** still refers to a complete failure or **DEBACLE**. Most observers believe that the government's and BP's **BELATED** (tardy, slow) response to the 2010 Gulf Oil Spill transformed a disaster into a devastating human-made **DEBACLE**.

147 | BOWDLERIZE
To remove or delete parts of a book, song, or other work that are considered offensive; to EXPURGATE (Word 156)

Dr. Thomas Bowdler, an English physician, thought parents should read Shakespeare's plays to their children. Although Shakespeare may be an immortal bard, his plays do contain profanity and suggestive scenes that may not be appropriate for family reading. So in 1818, Bowdler decided to publish a family edition of Shakespeare. In his preface, Bowdler noted that he carefully edited "those words and expressions which cannot, with propriety, be read aloud to a family." Outraged critics attacked Bowdler and **COINED** (Word 296) the new word **BOWDLERIZE** to describe the deletion of parts of a book or play that are deemed offensive. Interestingly, the **BOWDLERIZED** edition of Shakespeare proved to be a commercial success, thus, perhaps, vindicating Bowdler's judgment.

The controversy over **BOWDLERIZED** books did not end with Thomas Bowdler. In her book *The Language Police*, Diane Ravitch argues that American students are compelled to read bland texts that have been **BOWDLERIZED** by publishers and textbook committees who cut or change controversial material from books, even classics. For example, an anthology used in Tennessee schools changed "By God!" to "By gum!"

148 | GALVANIZE
To electrify; to stir into action as if with an electric shock

Luigi Galvani (1737–1790) was an Italian professor of physiology whose pioneering work stimulated important research into the nature of electricity. Galvani's name is still associated with an electrical process that puts a zinc coating over iron or steel.

One of the first uses of the word in a **FIGURATIVE** (metaphorical) sense is in Charlotte Bronte's 1853 novel *Villette*: "Her approach always **GALVANIZED** him to new and spasmodic life." In more recent times Rosa Parks's simple but powerful act of protest **GALVANIZED** the people of Montgomery, Alabama, to boycott the buses, thus giving additional **IMPETUS** (Word 78) to the Civil Rights Movement.

149 | PICAYUNE
Small value or importance; petty; trifling

The *New Orleans Times-Picayune* has one of the best-known and oddest names of an American newspaper. The word "picayune" originally referred to a small Spanish coin worth about six cents. Back in 1837, the original proprietors of the then *New Orleans Picayune* gave their new paper that name because a copy cost about six cents, or one picayune.

Today, the word **PICAYUNE** refers to something of small value and thus of little importance. After Hurricane Katrina, New Orleans leaders angrily accused FEMA officials of ignoring urgent problems while they focused on minor details that could best be described as **PICAYUNE**.

150 | GERRYMANDER

To divide a geographic area into voting districts so as to give unfair advantage to one party in elections

If you think the word **GERRYMANDER** sounds like the name of a strange political beast, you are right. The name was **COINED** (Word 296) by combining the word salamander, "a small lizard-like amphibian," with the last name of Elbridge Gerry, a former governor of Massachusetts. Gerry was immortalized in this word because an election district created by members of his party in 1812 looked like a salamander. When the famous artist Gilbert Stuart noticed the oddly-shaped district on a map in a newspaper editor's office, he decorated the outline of the district with a head, wings, and claws and then said to the editor, "That will do for a salamander!" "Gerrymander!" came the reply, and a new SAT word was **COINED** (Word 296).

Today, the word **GERRYMANDER** still retains its meaning of an oddly-shaped district designed to favor one party. For example, California has drawn district lines so that two pockets of Republican strength in Los Angeles separated by many miles were connected by a thin strip of coastline. In this way, most Republican voters were assigned to one **GERRYMANDERED** district. District 23 is one of the narrowest districts in the United States and is often referred to as "the district that disappears at high tide." **IRONICALLY** (Word 231), the seat has recently been held by a Democrat.

151 | MAVERICK

*An independent individual who does not go along with a group
or party; a nonconformist*

Samuel A. Maverick was one of the early leaders of Texas. He fought for
Texas independence, served as mayor of San Antonio, and eventually
purchased a 385,000-acre ranch. While Maverick's achievements have
been forgotten, his name is remembered because of his practice of
refusing to brand the cattle on his ranch. These unbranded cattle
were soon called *mavericks*.

Today, the meaning of the word **MAVERICK** has been extended from
cattle to people. A **MAVERICK** is anyone who doesn't follow the
common herd, thus a nonconformist. In the movie *Top Gun*, Lt. Peter
Mitchell received the nickname "Mav" because he was a nonconformist
who did not always follow the rules.

152 | JUGGERNAUT

An irresistible force that crushes everything in its path

Jagannath (or "Lord of the World") is an incarnation of the Hindu god
Vishnu. In the early 14th century, a Franciscan missionary named Friar
Odoric visited India. When he returned to Europe, Odoric published
a journal describing how Jagannath's devoted followers placed the
god's image on an enormous carriage which they pulled through
the streets. According to Odoric's inaccurate but sensational report,
excited worshippers threw themselves under the carriage and were
crushed to death. As Odoric's exaggerated story spread across Europe,
Jagannath's name was transformed into the new word **JUGGERNAUT**.

Today, the word **JUGGERNAUT** refers to an irresistible force that
crushes everything in its path. The D-Day assault forces were a
JUGGERNAUT that crushed the German defenses.

The Hunger Games' **JUGGERNAUT** continued to gain momentum with
the release of the first movie in China and on home entertainment.
Sales of the trilogy have become Amazon's best-selling series,
ECLIPSING (Word 295) the Harry Potter series.

153 | SERENDIPITY
Discovery by fortunate accident

Sri Lanka is an island off the southeast coast of India. Known to Arab geographers as Serendip, the exotic island was the setting of a fanciful Persian fairy tale, *The Three Princes of Serendip*. The story and its title inspired the English writer Horace Walpole (1717–1797) to **COIN** (Word 296) the word **SERENDIPITY**. In a letter written in 1754, Walpole explained that **SERENDIPITY** refers to the uncanny ability of the three princes to make chance discoveries.

Today, the word **SERENDIPITY** refers to an accidental but fortunate discovery. When Scottish physician Alexander Fleming went on vacation in 1928, he left a dish smeared with Staphylococcus bacteria on a bench in his laboratory. In his absence, a mold from another lab drifted onto the culture. When Fleming returned, he noticed that the bacteria had not grown where the mold had fallen. Fleming named the active ingredient in the mold penicillin. His **SERENDIPITOUS** discovery proved to be a **WATERSHED** (Word 268) event in modern medicine. Penicillin is still one of the most effective antibiotics used around the world.

154 | ZENITH
The highest point; the peak; the APEX

Arab astronomers called the point of the celestial sphere directly above the observer the *samt*, meaning "way of the head." When Muslims conquered the Iberian Peninsula, many Arabic words entered the Spanish language. Within a short time, the Arabic word *samt* became the Spanish word *zenit*. Over time, *zenit* passed into English and became **ZENITH**.

Today, the word **ZENITH** refers to the highest point or peak. On June 12, 1987, President Ronald Reagan spoke for the people of West Berlin and the entire Free World when he called upon Soviet leader Mikhail Gorbachev to tear down the Berlin Wall. Reagan's dramatic speech marked the **ZENITH** of his presidency and the beginning of the end of the Cold War.

155 | NADIR

The lowest point; the bottom

Arab astronomers called the point of the celestial sphere directly under the observer the *nazir*, or opposite. Thus, the phrase *nazir assant* meant "opposite of the zenith." With a slight modification, *nazir* entered the English language as **NADIR**.

Today the word **NADIR** is used to describe someone's (or something's) lowest point. In *The Dark Knight Rises*, Bruce Wayne's **NADIR** is when Bane physically cripples him and places him in The Pit, an essentially inescapable foreign prison, so that he must helplessly watch the destruction of Gotham on television. Defeated, filled with physical **ANGUISH** (Word 88), and forced to watch the annihilation of his beloved Gotham, Wayne is at his **NADIR** in The Pit. However, over several months, he slowly recovers from his injuries, regains his strength, escapes, and saves his city.

CHAPTER 5

The Mighty Little Affixes

156 – 205

An affix is a meaningful element added to a root in order to direct or change the root's meaning.

A <u>prefix</u> is a word part placed <u>before</u> a root. Prefixes are short but mighty. A knowledge of prefixes can help you unlock the meaning of difficult SAT words. Many vocabulary books contain long lists of Latin and Greek prefixes. Many like *ANTI* (against), *SUB* (under), and *MULTI* (many) are well-known and obvious. Still others, like *PERI* (around), generate few if any words tested on the SAT. This chapter will focus on five sets of the most widely-used prefixes on the SAT. Learning them is thus of **PARAMOUNT** (vital) importance.

A <u>suffix</u> is a word part that is added <u>to the end</u> of a root or word. We are including in this chapter a number of words ending with the suffix *–OUS*, by far the most useful suffix on the SAT.

A. *E* AND *EX*: THE MIGHTY PREFIXES *E* AND *EX* TELL YOU THAT THINGS ARE GOING OUT

The prefixes *E* and *EX* are **UBIQUITOUS** (Word 48). You are familiar with them in everyday words such as EXIT, EXTINGUISH, and ERASE. The prefixes *E* and *EX* always mean OUT. Here are seven frequently used SAT words that begin with the prefixes *E* and *EX*:

156 | EXPUNGE, EXCISE, EXPURGATE
To take OUT; to delete; to remove

In the movie *300*, Xerxes threatened to **EXPUNGE** all memory of Sparta and Leonidas: "Every piece of Greek parchment shall be burned, every Greek historian and every Greek scribe shall have his eyes put out and his thumbs cut off. Ultimately the very name of Sparta or Leonidas will be punishable by death. The world will never know you existed."

Xerxes failed to carry out his threat to **EXCISE** the names of Sparta and King Leonidas from the historic record. However, a powerful Egyptian Pharaoh, Thutmose III, did succeed in **EXPURGATING** the name of his stepmother, Hatshepsut, from Egyptian monuments. A female pharaoh, Hatshepsut reigned for nearly 20 years in the 15th century BCE. Possibly motivated by jealousy, Thutmose ruthlessly defaced his stepmother's monuments and **EXPURGATED** her name from historic records. All memory of Hatshepsut was lost until 19th century Egyptologists rediscovered her monuments and restored her place in history.

157 | ECCENTRIC
*Literally OUT of the center; departing from a recognized, conventional, or established norm; an odd, **UNCONVENTIONAL** (Word 7) person*

Who lives in a pineapple under the sea? SpongeBob SquarePants is very **ECCENTRIC** in his mannerisms. When he wants to blow a bubble or draw a circle, he always performs a strange procedure. To blow a perfect bubble, he spins around, double takes three times, and enacts a series of other weird motions. To draw a circle, he draws an entire front portrait and then erases all of the details. Although he might be a little **ECCENTRIC**, you can't argue with his results. SpongeBob always completes his work to perfection.

158 | EXTRICATE

To get OUT of a difficult situation or entanglement

Have you ever had to **EXTRICATE** yourself from an embarrassing situation? If so, you are not alone. In the movie *School of Rock*, Dewey Finn has to **EXTRICATE** himself from the embarrassing situation he created by impersonating his friend and claiming to be a certified elementary substitute teacher.

EXTRICATING yourself from a lie is embarrassing. However, being **EXTRICATED** from an automobile crash can be a matter of life or death. Fortunately, emergency workers have a number of tools specially designed to help **EXTRICATE** injured people from car wrecks and small spaces. These cutters, spreaders, and rams are collectively called "Jaws of Life."

159 | EXEMPLARY

Standing OUT from the norm; outstanding; worthy of imitation

Have you ever been praised for writing an **EXEMPLARY** report, giving an **EXEMPLARY** answer, or designing an **EXEMPLARY** project? If so, you should be proud of yourself. **EXEMPLARY** means to be outstanding and thus worthy of imitation. Recording artists and actors are recognized for their **EXEMPLARY** performances by receiving a VMA Moonman, a Grammy, or an Oscar. Scientists and writers are honored for their **EXEMPLARY** work by receiving a Nobel Prize.

160 | ENUMERATE
To count OUT; to list; to tick off the reasons for

What do Thomas Jefferson, the author of the Declaration of Independence, and Kat, the fictional character in *10 Things I Hate About You*, have in common? Both felt compelled to **ENUMERATE** the reasons for an action. In the Declaration of Independence, Jefferson **ENUMERATED** reasons why the colonies declared their independence from Great Britain. In a poem she read to her literature class, Kat **ENUMERATED** 10 reasons why she claimed to "hate" Patrick.

161 | ELUSIVE
OUT of reach and therefore difficult to catch, define, or describe

In *Indiana Jones and the Last Crusade*, Indiana Jones and his father search for the **ELUSIVE** Holy Grail. The Holy Grail is said to give eternal life, but it is hidden in an elaborate labyrinth. When Jones and his father arrive at the castle to obtain the Grail, Jones's father is fatally wounded and thus needs the Grail to survive. "Indy" solves a series of three difficult riddles, obtains the holy cup that has been **ELUSIVE** for so many years, and saves his father's life.

162 | EXORBITANT
Literally OUT of orbit and therefore unreasonably expensive

Serious competition in the NFL occurs both on and off the field. Football stadiums are being rebuilt, each one more lavish than the last. Cowboys Stadium is proof that not only are things bigger in Texas, they are also more **EXORBITANT**! The stadium features 300 luxury suites costing between $100,000 and $500,000 a year with a 20-year lease. Although this may seem **GRANDIOSE** (pretentious) to average fans, the suites provide "the ultimate football experience" by featuring limestone floors, private restrooms, and a special parking lot. The reserved parking is a **COVETED** (Word 32) feature. Parking is limited at Cowboys Stadium. As a result, regular football fans will pay $75 for parking, a price many are calling **EXORBITANT**.

B. *RE*: THE MIGHTY PREFIX *RE* TELLS YOU THAT THINGS ARE COMING BACK AGAIN AND AGAIN

The prefix *RE* means BACK or AGAIN. You are familiar with it in everyday words such as REPEAT, REWIND, and REVERSE. Here are 10 SAT words that begin with the prefix *RE*:

163 | REDUNDANT
Needlessly repetitive; saying things AGAIN and AGAIN

Tip for a Direct Hit

On the SAT the word REDUNDANCY usually refers to the duplication or repetition of equipment needed to provide a backup in case the primary systems fail. For example, scuba equipment includes a REDUNDANT regulator in case there is a problem with the main air regulator. This REDUNDANCY is an important safety precaution.

What do Justin Bieber and SAT teachers have in common? Both are **REDUNDANT** when they emphasize a key point. In his hit song *Baby*, JB **REDUNDANTLY** repeats the word "baby" an amazing 57 times. No wonder the song sticks in your mind! SAT teachers are also purposefully **REDUNDANT** when they **IMPLORE** (urge) their students to study the vocabulary words in *Direct Hits*. Here's why: a level 1 and 2 vocabulary will only enable you to achieve a critical reading score of about 450. You will need a level 3 vocabulary to achieve a score of about 580. Finally, you will need a level 4 and 5 vocabulary to score 600 and up. So now you know why SAT teachers are so **REDUNDANT**. Study your *Direct Hits* vocabulary!

164 | REPUDIATE, RECANT, RENOUNCE
To take BACK; to reject; to DISAVOW

"Martin, do you or do you not **REPUDIATE** these books and the falsehoods they contain?" The place was the Diet of Worms. The time was April 1521. The question posed by the papal legate Johann Eck required an answer. For Martin Luther, the moment of truth had finally arrived. How would Luther respond?

Luther refused to **REPUDIATE** his words, defiantly declaring, "I cannot, I will not **RECANT** these words. For to do so is to go against conscience. Here I stand!" Luther's courageous refusal to **RENOUNCE** his beliefs helped spark the Protestant Reformation.

165 | RELINQUISH
To surrender or give BACK (or return) a possession, right, or privilege

The Arab Spring is the name given to the revolutionary wave of demonstrations that began all over the Arab world in December 2010. In January 2011 in Egypt, after 18 days of angry mass protests, President Hosni Mubarak, the longest serving ruler in modern times (30 years), was forced to **RELINQUISH** his position. Power was transferred to the Supreme Council of the Armed Forces (SCAF), and Mubarak was tried and sentenced to life in prison for ordering the killing of peaceful demonstrators. In June 2012, after the first presidential election with more than one candidate since 2005, SCAF in turn **RELINQUISHED** its power to the newly-elected president, Mohammed Morsi.

166 | RESILIENT
Bouncing BACK from ADVERSITY or misfortune; recovering quickly

Amy's long wait for her SAT scores finally ended. She nervously accessed her College Board account. Then as the numbers appeared on her computer screen, her heart sank. The scores were not as good as she had hoped. What would Amy do? Would she make excuses and give up? Or would she be **RESILIENT** and bounce back from a temporary setback? Amy chose to study even harder. Her **RESILIENCE** worked. Her SAT scores shot up, and she received a scholarship to her top college choice.

Amy's story can be your story. The SAT is a challenging test. Don't be discouraged if your first results are not what you hoped for. Stay focused, study hard, and be **RESILIENT**!

167 | REAFFIRM

To assert AGAIN; to confirm; to state positively

Given at the height of the Cold War, John F. Kennedy's 1961 Inaugural Address **REAFFIRMED** his commitment to freedom when he pledged that America would "pay any price, bear any burden, meet any hardship, support any friend, oppose any foe to assure the survival and success of liberty." Given at the height of the Civil Rights Movement, Dr. King's "I Have A Dream" speech **REAFFIRMED** King's faith in the American dream: "I have a dream that my four little children will one day live in a nation where they will be judged not by the color of their skin but by the content of their character."

168 | RETICENT

Holding BACK one's thoughts, feelings and personal affairs; restrained or reserved

When Katie Holmes filed for divorce from Tom Cruise, media outlets speculated that the high-profile divorce would be an **ACRIMONIOUS** (Word 198) one. However, both Holmes and Cruise were **RETICENT** to discuss their feelings or the reasons behind the divorce, despite the media frenzy that followed. Tabloids published **LURID** (Word 313) stories about the couple's marriage, and media outlets featured dozens of **PUNDITS** (Word 117) offering their "expert" opinions and theories about the couple's divorce proceedings, prenuptial agreement, and religious beliefs. Less than two weeks after Holmes filed for divorce, the couple reached a settlement and issued a statement that confirmed their **RETICENCE** to speak about their personal affairs, saying, "We want to keep matters affecting our family private."

On July 20, 1969, the first man to step onto the surface of the moon, astronaut Neil Armstrong, issued some of the most memorable **APHORISMS** (Word 434) of the 20th century: "Houston: Tranquility Base here. The *Eagle* has landed. " and "That's one small step for [a] man, one giant leap for mankind." However, he was also known for his **RETICENCE**. Even though he was **REVERED** (deeply respected or admired) as a hero and was awarded the Presidential Medal of Freedom for his work, he refused to give interviews, sign autographs, or make public appearances.

169 | REBUFF

To repel or drive BACK; to bluntly reject

In the movie *Superman Returns*, Lois Lane **REBUFFS** Superman when she writes an article entitled, "Why the World Doesn't Need Superman." In the movie *Clueless*, Cher claims that Mr. Hall "brutally **REBUFFED**" her plea that he raise her debate grade. In her song "Your Love Is My Drug," Ke$ha remains **RECALCITRANT** (Word 15) as she **REBUFFS** all advice from her friends and family about breaking up with her boyfriend. She says she "won't listen to any advice," even though "momma's telling me I should think twice."

170 | RENOVATE

To make new AGAIN (see Word 126); to restore by repairing and remodeling

NOV is a Latin root meaning "new." **RENOVATE** thus means to make new again. Hurricane Katrina caused extensive damage in New Orleans and Biloxi, Mississippi. Business and community leaders in both cities have vowed to undertake extensive **RENOVATION** projects to restore damaged neighborhoods and revive tourism. For example, in 2007, actor Brad Pitt commissioned 13 architecture firms to submit designs for homes to help **RENOVATE** New Orleans' **IMPOVERISHED** (Word 257) Lower Ninth Ward. The project, called *Make It Right*, calls for building 150 affordable, environmentally-sound homes. By June 2012 they had already completed 75 of the houses.

171 | REJUVENATE

To make young AGAIN; to restore youthful vigor and appearance

Tip for a Direct Hit

The word REJUVENATE is formed by combining the prefix *RE* meaning "again" and the Latin root *juvenis* meaning "young." So REJUVENATE literally means to be young again.

REJUVENATE is an enticing word. Everyone wants to look and feel young. Health spas promise to **REJUVENATE** exhausted muscles, shampoos promise to **REJUVENATE** tired hair, and herbal medicines promise to **REJUVENATE** worn-out immune systems.

172 | RESURGENT

Rising AGAIN; sweeping or surging BACK

Apple Computer was founded on April 1, 1976. After great initial success, the company suffered crippling financial losses. However, Apple proved to be **RESILIENT** (Word 166), starting in 1998 with the release of the iMac computer, which featured a unique design and new technology. Over the following years, the **RESURGENT** company introduced a series of **INNOVATIVE** (Word 126) and popular products that included the iPod, the iPhone, and the iPad. With its commitment to **INNOVATION** and sleek design, Apple has risen to be the most profitable technology company in the world.

173 | REPUGNANT

ABHORRENT; offensive to the mind or senses; causing distaste or AVERSION

What do a bad smell, cheating on an exam, and cannibalism have in common? They are all **REPUGNANT** to us, either physically or morally. Things that some people may find **REPUGNANT** are other people's political views, the use of animals in scientific experiments, and the eating of meat. Many consider the Confederate flag a **REPUGNANT** symbol of slavery.

In the movie *Animal House*, one of the most iconic raunchy comedies, smug Omega fraternity president Greg Marmalard describes the activities of the Delta House with **REPUGNANCE**: "A Roman toga party was held, from which we have received two dozen reports of individual acts of perversion so profound and disgusting that decorum prohibits listing them here."

KNOW YOUR ROOTS		
LATIN ROOT: ***PUGN,*** ***PUG***	fighting (from ***pugnus***, a fist)	PUGNACIOUS — disposed to fight, quarrelsome, combative PUGILIST — a boxer, one who fights with his fists REPUGNANCE — fighting back, extreme dislike, AVERSION, disgust, ANTIPATHY IMPUGN — to fight against, attack, challenge the motives of

C. *DE*: THE MIGHTY PREFIX *DE* TELLS YOU THAT THINGS ARE HEADED DOWN, DOWN, DOWN

The prefix *DE* means DOWN. You are familiar with *DE* in such every-day words as DEMOLISH, DECLINE, and DEPRESS. Here are eight SAT words that begin with the prefix *DE*:

174 | DELETERIOUS
Going DOWN in the sense of having a harmful effect; injurious

What do you think is the fastest growing cause of disease and death in America? The surprising and tragic answer is obesity. As a result of being **SEDENTARY** (lacking physical activity) and practicing unhealthy eating habits, an **UNPRECEDENTED** (Word 285) number of Americans are carrying excess body weight. This excess weight can have a number of **DELETERIOUS** effects, including heart disease, asthma, and diabetes.

A tragic series of recent teen suicides has revealed the **DELETERIOUS** effects of bullying. The **PREVALENCE** (Word 48) of bullying in schools and on the internet has created a **NOXIOUS** (Word 323) environment for children and teenagers. In response to the tragedies, the media is shedding light on bullying and its **DELETERIOUS** effects. ABC Family created a campaign called Delete Digital Drama in order to help end cyberbullying. The Cartoon Network has also started a campaign called Stop Bullying Speak Up, which teaches children what to do when they observe instances of bullying. Lady Gaga has spoken out about her experience with bullying and has vowed to make bullying illegal.

175 | DECRY
To put DOWN in the sense of openly condemning; to express strong disapproval

During the 1920s, American novelists such as Sinclair Lewis **DECRIED** the era's rampant materialism and conformity. Three decades later, Jack Kerouac and other Beat Generation writers also **DECRIED** sterile middle-class conformity while celebrating spontaneous individualism and creativity through their **BOHEMIAN** (characteristic of artists or intellectuals who live without regard for conventional rules) lifestyles.

176 | DESPONDENT, MOROSE
DOWNCAST; very dejected; FORLORN

No character is as **DESPONDENT** as Eeyore from *Winnie the Pooh*. An old gray donkey, Eeyore is characterized by his mopey and pessimistic nature. Just look at how Eeyore feels about his birthday:

"*After all, what are birthdays? Here today and gone tomorrow.***"**

You have to feel bad for **DESPONDENT** Eeyore if he can't even enjoy his own birthday! Luckily, his friends Pooh, Tigger, and Piglet help to **ALLEVIATE** (Word 31) his **MOROSE** mood.

During their 19 years together, Mumtaz Mahal gave Emperor Shah Jahan 14 children. When she suddenly died during childbirth, Shah

Jahan was grief-stricken. The now **MOROSE** emperor canceled all appointments and refused to eat or drink for eight days. One historian recorded that when Mumtaz Mahal died, the emperor was in danger of dying himself. When he finally recovered, Shah Jahan built the Taj Mahal as a mausoleum for his beloved wife.

177 | DENOUNCE

To put DOWN in the sense of a making a formal accusation; to speak against

The pages of history contain a number of inspiring examples of brave individuals who **DENOUNCED** corruption, tyranny, and moral abuses. Voltaire **DENOUNCED** the Old Regime in France, William Lloyd Garrison **DENOUNCED** slavery, Rachel Carson **DENOUNCED** the use of chemical pesticides, and Nelson Mandela **DENOUNCED** apartheid.

178 | DEMISE

Sent DOWN in the sense of ending in death; the cessation of existence or activity

What do the dinosaurs and the Whig Party have in common? Each met with a sudden and unexpected **DEMISE**. Paleontologists now believe that a giant asteroid struck the Earth about 65 million years ago, causing the **DEMISE** of the dinosaurs and many other plants and animals. Historians point out that the Kansas–Nebraska Act of 1854 brought about the final **DEMISE** of the Whig Party while at the same time sparking the rise of the Republican Party. Note that the word **DEMISE** is formed by combining the prefix *DE* meaning "down" with the Latin root *MISS* meaning "to send" (see KNOW YOUR ROOTS p. 47). So **DEMISE** literally means "to send down."

179 | DEBUNK
To put DOWN by exposing false and exaggerated claims

Because the public has always been fascinated by the lives of celebrities, publishers have made a fortune by capitalizing on this interest and producing magazines and tabloids filled with **LURID** (Word 313) gossip and rumors. In the past, celebrities have been helpless in **DEBUNKING** these rumors. Today, however, celebrities have found Twitter to be a useful way to **DEBUNK** the myths and **HEARSAY** (rumors) about their lives. Justin Bieber tweeted, "correcting rumors… #ilovetwitter." Talk about Jennifer Aniston's personal life constantly swirls about the internet and gossip magazines. Aniston once joked, "I should get a Twitter account just for rumor control."

180 | DERIDE, DERISIVE
To put DOWN with contemptuous jeering; to ridicule or laugh at

The long-running animated sitcom *South Park* is famous for its **DERISIVE** approach to all aspects of society, from the government to religions to celebrities like Tom Cruise, Kanye West, and the *Jersey Shore* cast. The **ICONOCLASTIC** (Word 107) show's creators Trey Parker and Matt Stone refuse to be **DEFERENTIAL** (Word 216) to any subject, and they call themselves "equal opportunity offenders." No subject is sacred enough to escape being **SATIRIZED** (Word 233) on the **IRREVERENT** (Word 187) comedy. *South Park*'s **DERISIVE** tone is set through this **FACETIOUS** (Word 362) disclaimer that airs before each episode: "All characters and events in this show—even those based on real people—are entirely fictional. All celebrity voices are impersonated… poorly. The following program contains coarse language and due to its content should not be viewed by anyone."

DERISION is not limited to the television shows. New artistic styles have often been **DERIDED** by both the public and critics. For example, Edouard Manet's painting "Luncheon on the Grass" provoked a storm of scorn and **DERISION**. Hostile critics were **DERISIVE**, calling Manet an "apostle of the ugly and repulsive."

181 | DEVOID

DOWN in the sense of being empty; completely lacking in substance or quality; BEREFT; vacant

What is the worst movie you have ever seen? Why did you select this movie? You probably chose the movie because it was **DEVOID** of humor, plot, and decent acting. Here is a list of movies that were panned by critics for being **DEVOID** of all redeeming value: *Battlefield Earth, Gigli, Godzilla, From Justin to Kelly, Glitter, Speed Racer, Jack and Jill, One For The Money.*

D. *IM, IN* AND *IR*: THESE MIGHTY LATIN PREFIXES ALL TELL YOU NO OR NOT

The prefixes *IM, IN, IR,* and *IL* are actually different forms of the same prefix: *IN*, which means NO or NOT. You are familiar with this prefix in everyday words such as INCOMPETENT, IMMATURE, IRREPLACEABLE, and ILLEGAL. See p. 100 for five other prefixes that also exist in different forms. Here are seven words that begin with variations of the prefix *IN*.

182 | IMPECCABLE

Having NO flaws; perfect

Look closely at the word **IMPECCABLE**. The prefix IM means "no," and the Latin verb *peccare* means "to sin." So the word **IMPECCABLE** literally means to have no sin and thus to be flawless or perfect.

Do you open doors for your girlfriend and say "yes, sir" and "yes, ma'am" when speaking to adults? If so, you are demonstrating **IMPECCABLE** manners. Do you complete your homework assignments in advance and study for all your tests? If so, you are demonstrating **IMPECCABLE** judgment. Whether manners or judgment, **IMPECCABLE** always means flawless. You can also show **IMPECCABLE** taste and dress **IMPECCABLY**.

183 | IMPLACABLE
*NOT capable of being **PLACATED** (Word 390) or appeased*

In his quest to fight for "truth, justice, and the American way," Superman must defeat Lex Luther and other **IMPLACABLE** foes. Superman is not alone in his struggle against **IMPLACABLE** villains. Spider-Man must defeat the Green Goblin, and Batman's most **IMPLACABLE** enemy is the Joker.

In the *Twilight* **SAGA** (Word 236), the Cullens must deal with the powerful and **IMPLACABLE** Volturi coven of vampires. The Volturi, the unofficial royalty of the vampire world, pride themselves on their ability to rule all other vampires. The Volturi envy the gifts and abilities of the Cullen vampires and fear their growing strength. Though the Cullens try to appease the Volturi by obeying the laws governing the vampire world, the **IMPLACABLE** Volturi will not rest until the Cullen clan has been disbanded.

184 | INEXORABLE
NOT capable of being stopped; relentless; inevitable

Although it was a luxury liner, the Titanic did not have the advanced warning systems that modern ships have today. The Titanic did have six lookout guards who stood in the crow's nest and kept a **VIGILANT** (watchful, alert) lookout for passing icebergs that could endanger the ship. At 11:40 p.m. on April 15, 1912, Frederick Fleet suddenly spotted an iceberg directly in the ship's path. Fleet urgently informed the bridge, and frantic officers ordered emergency maneuvers. But the ship was traveling too fast. It was on an **INEXORABLE** course to hit the iceberg. The Titanic sank 2 hours and 40 minutes after Fleet's fateful warning.

185 | INCOHERENT

NOT coherent and therefore lacking organization; lacking logical or meaningful connections

One of the most **INCOHERENT** statements ever recorded was uttered in 2007 by a contestant in the Miss Teen USA Pageant. The contestant was told that a recent poll showed that one-fifth of Americans cannot locate the United States on a map. She was asked to explain why. Here is her response in all of its **INCOHERENT** glory:

"*I personally believe that U.S. Americans are unable to do so because, uh, some ... people out there in our nation don't have maps and, uh, I believe that our, uh, education like such as in South Africa and, uh, the Iraq, everywhere like such as, and, I believe that they should, our education over HERE in the U.S. should help the U.S., uh, or, uh, should help South Africa and should help the Iraq and the Asian countries, so we will be able to build up our future, for our children.***"**

She later explained that she was flustered by the question and possibly redeemed herself by re-answering the question more coherently on television.

186 | INSURMOUNTABLE

NOT capable of being surmounted or overcome

Beginning in the 1850s, far-seeing American leaders dreamed of building a transcontinental railroad that would bind the nation together. But **SKEPTICS** (Word 102) argued that while the railroad was a worthy goal, it would face a series of **INSURMOUNTABLE** obstacles that included hostile Plains Indians and the towering, snow-clogged Sierra Nevada mountains. Crews that at times included over 15,000 workers repelled the Indians and blasted tunnels through the mountains. The once **INSURMOUNTABLE** task was completed when Leland Stanford used a silver sledge-hammer to drive in the final golden spike on May 10, 1869.

187 | IRREVERENT

Lacking proper respect or seriousness; disrespectful

Even though they go to church every Sunday and pray at the dinner table before many meals, the TV Simpson family members are well-known for their **IRREVERENT** jokes and witticisms. Journalist Mark Pinsky wrote: "*The Simpsons* is consistently **IRREVERENT** toward organized religion's failings and excesses."

Here is one example of an **IRREVERENT** discussion with God.

Homer to God:	*"I'm not a bad guy. I work hard and I love my kids. So why should I spend half my Sunday hearing about how I'm going to hell?"*
God:	*"Hmm, you've got a point there. You know sometimes even I'd rather be watching football."*

Here is another:

"Dear God, this is Marge Simpson. If you stop this hurricane and save our family, we will be forever grateful and recommend you to all our friends."

188 | IRRESOLUTE

*NOT **RESOLUTE** (Word 359); uncertain how to act or proceed; **INDECISIVE; VACILLATING** (Word 371)*

Hamlet's father's ghost has assigned Hamlet the task of avenging his father's murder. He knows that his uncle Claudius is the murderer, and he has plenty of opportunity, but since he is an **IRRESOLUTE** and **MELANCHOLY** (gloomy) character given to obsessive brooding, he tends to overanalyze the situation to such a degree that he cannot act. Instead, he **IRRESOLUTELY** thinks, debates, delays, and seeks further proof. Finally, disgusted by his own feeble **IRRESOLUTION**, he observes the Norwegian prince Fortinbras, who with much less cause is engaged in much more action. He ends this famous soliloquy with the **RESOLUTE** declaration: "O, from this time forth, My thoughts be bloody or be nothing worth!"

KNOW YOUR LATIN PREFIXES

In the course of the expansion of the Roman Empire and the relaxation of pronunciation over time, many Latin prefixes that end with a consonant often (but not always) changed their spelling to match the first letter of the roots to which they were attached. This process is called ASSIMILATION, because the root assimilates the prefix and the neighboring sounds become similar. Some other examples of such prefixes, besides *IN-*, are below.

AD- **to, toward**
ACCURATE—done with care, exact
AFFECT—to do something to, to have influence on
ANNOTATE—to add notes to
ADVENTURE—to take a risk, venture toward
(*Ad-* does not assimilate here before the v)

COM- **with**
COLLOQUIUM—a speaking together
COMMIT—to send with
(*Com-* does not need to change here)
CORRUPT—to break with, spoil

DIS- **apart**
DIFFER—to set apart
DISPEL—to push in different directions

OB- **against, toward**
OFFER—to bring toward, to present
OCCUR—to run against, to happen

SUB- **under, up from below**
SUFFER—to carry under
SUGGEST—to bring up
SUBTITLE—a subordinate or additional title
(*Sub-* does not assimilate here)

E. *CIRCU*: WHAT GOES AROUND COMES AROUND

The prefix *CIRCU* means AROUND. You are familiar with it in everyday words such as CIRCUMFERENCE, CIRCUIT, and CIRCULATION. Here are four SAT words that begin with the prefix *CIRCU*:

189 | CIRCUMSPECT

Looking carefully AROUND—thus cautious and careful;
PRUDENT; discreet

In Homer's *Odyssey*, Penelope cautiously refuses to recognize the much-changed returned Odysseus until he describes their bed, which was built around an olive tree, its trunk functioning as one of the bedposts. No one but her husband would know this fact. Hearing this, the cautious and **CIRCUMSPECT** Penelope is persuaded of the stranger's identity and joyfully welcomes him home.

In Shakespeare's *Hamlet*, Laertes cautions his sister Ophelia to be more **CIRCUMSPECT** in her dealings with Hamlet, a prince whose will is not his own. Laertes says," Then weigh what loss your honor may sustain/ If with too credent ear you list his songs.... Be wary then; best safety lies in fear." Then Polonius, Ophelia and Laertes's father, **REITERATES** (repeats) the same message, ordering her: "Be somewhat scanter of your maiden presence." He hopes that such **CIRCUMSPECTION** will protect her from being dishonored and abandoned.

190 | CIRCUITOUS

CIRCULAR and therefore indirect in language, behavior, or action, roundabout

In the movie *National Treasure: Book of Secrets*, Benjamin Franklin Gates' great-great grandfather is suddenly implicated as a key conspirator in Abraham Lincoln's death. Determined to prove his ancestor's innocence, Ben follows a chain of clues that leads him on a **CIRCUITOUS** chase that begins in Paris and then takes him to Buckingham Palace in London, the White House, a secret tunnel under Mount Vernon, the Library of Congress, and finally Mount Rushmore. On this **CIRCUITOUS** journey Ben and his crew uncover a number of startling revelations and secrets.

A **CIRCUIT** is a circular course or journey, like that of the earth around the sun.

191 | CIRCUMVENT

To circle AROUND and therefore bypass; to avoid by artful maneuvering

During the 1920s, Al Capone and other gangsters built profitable illegal businesses by **CIRCUMVENTING** prohibition laws. Today, illegal businesses continue to **CIRCUMVENT** our laws. For example, drug lords annually smuggle over 100 tons of cocaine and other illegal drugs into the United States.

Sometimes nations **CIRCUMVENT** international law. Iran signed the Nuclear Non-Proliferation Treaty in 1970. Nonetheless, many believe that the Iranian government is now **CIRCUMVENTING** the international agreements by secretly developing a program to build nuclear weapons.

192 | CIRCUMSCRIBE
To draw a line AROUND and therefore to narrowly limit or restrict actions

What do Juliet (*Romeo and Juliet*), Janie Crawford (*Their Eyes Were Watching God*), and Viola Hastings (*She's The Man*) have in common? Although they live in very different times and places, all face restrictions that **CIRCUMSCRIBE** their freedom. Juliet wants to marry Romeo but can't because her family **CIRCUMSCRIBES** her freedom by insisting she marry Count Paris. Janie wants to socialize with a variety of people but can't because her husband **CIRCUMSCRIBES** her freedom by refusing to let her participate in the rich social life that occurs on the front porch of their general store. And Viola wants to try out for the boys soccer team but can't because the coach **CIRCUMSCRIBES** her freedom by contending that girls aren't good enough to play with boys.

F. *-OUS*: THIS ALL-IMPORTANT SUFFIX MEANS FILLED WITH OR HAVING THE QUALITIES OF

The suffix *-OUS* means FILLED WITH or HAVING THE QUALITIES OF. You are familiar with it in everyday words such as JOYOUS, COURAGEOUS, and POISONOUS. Here are 13 SAT words that end with the suffix *-OUS*:

193 | MAGNANIMOUS
FILLED WITH generosity and forgiveness; forgoing resentment and revenge

On first glance, **MAGNANIMOUS** looks like a "big" and difficult SAT word. But looks can be deceiving. Let's use our knowledge of prefixes, roots, and the suffix -*OUS* to divide and conquer **MAGNANIMOUS**!

The prefix *MAGNA* is easy to recognize. It means "big" as in the word **MAGNIFY**. The root *ANIM* comes from the Latin *animex* meaning "breath" or soul. An animal is thus a living, breathing thing, and an inanimate object lacks a spirit. And finally, the suffix -*OUS* means "is filled with" or "having the qualities of." So **MAGNANIMOUS** literally means "filled with a great spirit" and therefore generous and forgiving. For example, following Lee's surrender at Appomattox, Grant **MAGNANIMOUSLY** allowed the Confederate officers to keep their side arms and permitted soldiers to keep personal horses and mules. The Union troops then **MAGNANIMOUSLY** saluted as their defeated foes marched past them.

194 | ERRONEOUS
FILLED WITH errors; wrong

Lil Wayne's **PENCHANT** (Word 62) for tattoos is well known. Fascinated fans have deciphered the meaning of most of Wheezy's **MYRIAD** (Word 352) tats. However, the three teardrops on his face remain a source of controversy. Many believe that they represent people Lil Wayne has killed. This belief is **ERRONEOUS** and totally **UNCORROBORATED** (unsupported). In his song "Hustler Musik," Wheezy clearly states that he has never killed anyone. The three teardrops actually represent family members who have been killed.

195 | MOMENTOUS
FILLED WITH importance; very significant

In 1960 lunch counters throughout the South remained segregated. While moderates urged patience, Joe McNeil and three other black college students disagreed. Calling segregation "evil pure and simple," the four students sat down at a Woolworth's lunch counter in Greensboro, North Carolina, and ordered coffee and apple pie. Although the waitress refused to serve them, the students remained **STEADFAST** (fixed, unswerving) in their determination to desegregate the dining area. Now known as the Greensboro Four, the students ultimately prevailed. The sit-in movement begun by the Greensboro Four had **MOMENTOUS** consequences. Just four years later, the Civil Rights Act of 1964 **MANDATED** (ordered) desegregation in all public places.

196 | MELLIFLUOUS
Smooth and sweet; flowing like honey

Let's divide and conquer the seemingly difficult SAT word, **MELLIFLUOUS**. The Latin roots *MEL* meaning "honey" and *FLUUS* meaning "flow" are the key to understanding **MELLIFLUOUS**. **MELLIFLUOUS** is literally "filled with flowing honey." It almost always is used to describe singers who have sweet-sounding voices. For example, Smokey Robinson, Marvin Gaye, Otis Redding, and Usher are all renowned for their smooth, **MELLIFLUOUS** voices.

197 | OMINOUS
FILLED WITH menace; threatening

An omen is a sign indicating that something good or bad will happen. The word **OMINOUS** is filled with bad omens that **PORTEND** (foretell) the imminent arrival of something that will be both menacing and threatening. For example, scientists warn that melting glaciers, rising sea levels, and rising temperatures are all **OMINOUS** signs that global warming is getting worse at an alarming rate.

198 | ACRIMONIOUS

FILLED WITH bitterness; sharpness in words; RANCOROUS

Tip for a Direct Hit

ACUTE, ACUITY, and EXACERBATE (Word 277) also are related to the Latin *ACER*. ACUTE refers to a sharp feeling or sense, such as an acute sense of smell. ACUITY means keenness or sharp-sightedness. EXACERBATE means to make a problem sharper and thus worse.

What do the words **ACRIMONIOUS**, **ACID**, **ACRID** (Word 211), and **ACERBIC** (Word 211) have in common? All four are derived from the Proto-Indo-European root *AK-*, which means "to be sharp, to rise to a point, to pierce." From that ancient source we get the Latin adjective *ACER* (masculine form), *ACRIS* (feminine), *ACRE* (neuter) meaning sharp, pungent, bitter, eager, and fierce, as well as *ACIDUS*, meaning sharp and sour.

Celebrity divorces often degenerate into **ACRIMONIOUS** contests over money and child custody. While the couples do not throw acid at each other, they often don't hesitate to hurl **ACRIMONIOUS** accusations at their spouses. For example, Denise Richards alleged that Charlie Sheen was "unfaithful and abusive," while Britney Spears called Kevin Federline "the biggest mistake I've ever made." Needless to say, celebrity magazines are only too happy to **CHRONICLE** (record) all the **ACRIMONIOUS** allegations made by the stars and their lawyers.

199 | COPIOUS

FILLED WITH abundance; plentiful

What do the Greek god Zeus, the Thanksgiving horn of plenty, the SAT word **COPIOUS**, and *The Hunger Games* have in common? According to Greek mythology, the cornucopia refers to the horn of a goat that nursed Zeus. The horn had supernatural powers and soon became a symbol of fertility and plenty. In America, the cornucopia has come to be associated with the Thanksgiving harvest. The SAT word **COPIOUS** is derived from the Latin word *copia* meaning "plenty," so **COPIOUS** means filled with plenty and abundant. In *The Hunger Games*, the arena features a giant horn called the Cornucopia that contains **COPIOUS** amounts of weapons, food, medicine, and other survival equipment. When the Games begin, many of the tributes race to the Cornucopia to fight each other for the best supplies.

200 | ABSTEMIOUS
*FILLED WITH moderation; **TEMPERATE** (Word 89) in eating and drinking*

ABS is a Latin prefix meaning "away or off." For example, absent students are away from school. The Latin word *temetum* means an intoxicating drink. So if you are **ABSTEMIOUS**, you are filled with a desire to stay away from strong drinks. Today, an **ABSTEMIOUS** person can also be moderate or **TEMPERATE** in eating.

201 | MALODOROUS
FILLED WITH an unpleasant odor; foul-smelling

What do stink bugs and skunks have in common? Both can **EMIT** (give off) a **MALODOROUS** smell. If disturbed, stink bugs emit a liquid whose **MALODOROUS** smell is due to cyanide compounds. Skunks are notorious for their **MALODOROUS** scent glands, which emit a highly offensive smell usually described as a combination of the odors of rotten eggs, garlic, and burnt rubber. The skunk's **MALODOROUS** smell is a defensive weapon that repels predators and can be detected up to a mile away.

202 | TEDIOUS
FILLED WITH boredom; very tiresome; dull and fatiguing

What do studying long lists of vocabulary words and taking practice tests have in common? Most students find these tasks very **TEDIOUS**. *Direct Hits* is designed to make studying vocabulary much less **TEDIOUS**. In fact, we hope that you have found Volume 1 to be an interesting learning experience that has helped you speak more eloquently, write more convincingly, and, of course, score higher on your tests!

203 | HEINOUS, EGREGIOUS

Flagrantly, conspicuously bad; abominable; shockingly evil; monstrous; outrageous

HEINOUS crimes are those that are revolting to the average person, often referred to as Crimes of Moral **TURPITUDE** (evil). Perhaps the most **INFAMOUS** (widely but unfavorably known) **PERPETRATOR** (person who commits a bad act) of **HEINOUS** acts was Adolf Hitler, the German Nazi implementer of the crimes of the Holocaust.

EGREGIOUS acts are not quite as stunningly monstrous as to be **HEINOUS**, but they are still shockingly bad. Doping in sports is considered one of the most **EGREGIOUS** things an athlete can do, particularly at the Olympics. Athletes can face public warnings, sanctions, and even lifetime bans for the most **EGREGIOUS** cases. They can be sent home in disgrace and stripped of their Olympic medals.

You can use **EGREGIOUS** in a slightly **HYPERBOLIC** (Word 234) way, too, so that you might refer to **EGREGIOUS** grammar errors or **EGREGIOUS** handwriting.

204 | GRATUITOUS

Unwarranted; not called for by the circumstances; unnecessary

Artistic works, like movies or novels, are sometimes criticized for containing **GRATUITOUS**, or unnecessary, scenes that do not seem **INTRINSIC** (essential) to the work but seem to be included merely to **TITILLATE** (excite pleasurably) the audience or sell more tickets. For instance, many feel that the violence in Quentin Tarantino's films, such as *Kill Bill*, is over the top and **TANGENTIAL** (only superficially relevant, digressive) to the plot. Many horror movies have been criticized for scenes of **GRATUITOUS** sex and nudity.

On another note, the original meaning of **GRATUITY** was a tip, something extra, not necessary or required but given freely to a waiter, porter, or driver as an extra payment for services rendered. These days a **GRATUITY** is usually expected and is sometimes even added to the bill.

205 | PRECARIOUS, PERILOUS
| *Uncertain; characterized by a lack of security or stability*

Climbing Mt. Everest, the world's highest mountain, with a peak at 8,850 meters (29,035 ft) above sea level, is **PRECARIOUS** in the best of conditions. Recently climbers have encountered even more **PERILOUS** conditions with the light snowfall, steep icy slopes, and low oxygen levels, as well as a human "traffic jam" between the last staging camp and the summit, aptly named the "death zone." At the end of the 2012 hiking season an estimated 150 climbers rushed to take advantage of a short window of good weather, creating even more **PRECARIOUS** conditions and causing the deaths of at least four climbers.

Since the economic crash in 2008 many Americans have found themselves in a **PRECARIOUS** financial situation. For the first time student loan debt has **SURPASSED** (to go beyond) credit card debt, 40 percent of homes in the U.S. are now worth less than the mortgage debt, and the job market continues to be weak.

CHAPTER 6

Name That Tone/ Watch That Attitude | *206 – 225*

On every PSAT, SAT, and AP English exam there are questions that ask about an author's **ATTITUDE**, the author's or speaker's TONE, or the MOOD of a passage. The attitude, tone, or mood can be identified by examining the language and word choices in a passage. One way to think about TONE is that it is very akin to TONE OF VOICE.

To determine the tone of a passage, you may find these steps helpful:

1. Underline the descriptive words in the passage. These can be adjectives, adverbs, verbs, and nouns.
2. Identify the connotations of these words. Are they positive or negative? Or perhaps neutral?
3. Characterize the feelings the connotations generate.
4. Decide if there are hints that the speaker may not really mean everything he or she says. Such **NUANCES** (Word 361) might lead you to identify an **IRONIC** (Word 231) tone.
5. Visualize the expression on the speaker's face, for instance a **WRY** (Word 6) smile or a contemptuous smirk.
6. Listen to the passage. What is the author's TONE OF VOICE?

In addition to the tone words you have already encountered, like **AMBIVALENT** (Word 1), **SARCASTIC** (Word 3), and **NOSTALGIC** (Word 23), we have included 20 additional tone words that have appeared on recent tests.

206 | WISTFUL

*Longing and yearning, tinged with **MELANCHOLY** (long-lasting sadness) and **PENSIVENESS** (Word 214)*

Legions of Harry Potter fans **WISTFULLY** prepared to watch the final film *Harry Potter and The Deathly Hallows–Part 2*. A 14-year bond developed between the readers and the characters as many fans between the ages of 14 and 24 grew up along with Harry, Ron, and Hermione. These devotees compare the end of the series to the end of their childhood.

In preparation for the **EPIC** (Word 236) finale, many fans conducted their own **NOSTALGIC** (Word 23) **RETROSPECTIVES** (surveys of past events) by either rereading J.K. Rowling's novels or revisiting the film adaptations. One fan **WISTFULLY** summed it up this way: "Harry Potter is a once-in-a-generation event."

207 | EARNEST

*Serious in intention or purpose; showing depth and **SINCERITY** of feelings*

Adele wrote her song "Rolling in the Deep" on the same day she broke up with her boyfriend. The lyrics display Adele's **SINCERE** (genuine) belief that their relationship could have been very special.

We could have had it all
Rolling in the deep
You had my heart inside of your hand
And you played it to the beat

When asked how she felt about her breakup, Adele did not sugarcoat the truth. She spoke **EARNESTLY**: "I was really, really angry with my personal life up to about a year ago. I've grown up a little as well, and I like to think I've blossomed into who I'm going to become."

Adele certainly did move on successfully. In May 2011 her song "Rolling in the Deep" became her first #1 hit!

208 | DISGRUNTLED, DISCONTENTED

Angry; dissatisfied; annoyed; impatient; irritated

Some of the top companies in the world work tirelessly to make sure that their employees are not **DISGRUNTLED**. After all, happy employees are more productive than **DISCONTENTED** employees. Google is exceptionally notable for the benefits it provides its employees. At the Googleplex office in Mountain View, California, employees bring their pets to work, receive complimentary gourmet meals, have gym and pool access, and much more. It is clear that Google doesn't want its employees to be **DISGRUNTLED**.

209 | AUTHORITATIVE

Commanding and self-confident; likely to be respected and obeyed, based on competent authority

In the film *DodgeBall: A True Underdog Story*, Peter LaFleur must compete and win a dodgeball tournament to save his business, a gym called Average Joe's. The employees of Average Joe's rally together to form an amateur dodgeball team. They enlist the help of Patches O'Houlihan, an **AUTHORITATIVE** figure, to train and lead the team. Patches improves the dodgeball team through some **UNORTHODOX** (Word 7) methods: throwing wrenches at the team, forcing them to dodge oncoming cars, and constantly **DERIDING** (Word 180) them with insults. Patches' **AUTHORITATIVE** manner inspires the Average Joe's team to victory and ultimately saves the gym.

210 | FRIVOLITY

*The trait of being **FRIVOLOUS**; not serious or sensible*

FRIVOLOUS

Lacking any serious purpose or value; given to trifling or levity

One form of **FRIVOLOUS** spending that has become **UBIQUITOUS** (Word 48) is bottled water. Many bottled water companies simply sell municipal water; you can get the same water from your tap. Also, if not properly recycled, disposable water bottles contribute to **FRIVOLOUS** waste. The 30 billion plastic water bottles that are thrown away each year can take thousands of years to decompose. Using a reusable water bottle or canteen reduces **FRIVOLOUS** consumption, saves money, and protects the environment.

211 | ACERBIC, ACRID
Harsh, bitter, sharp, CAUSTIC (Word 242)

ACERBIC and **ACRID** both refer to the sharp and corrosive tone displayed by acid-tongued critics. **ACRID** can also refer to an unpleasantly **PUNGENT** (sharp) smell or taste. *Glee*'s cheerleading coach Sue Sylvester is famous for her **ACERBIC** comments directed at everyone around her. In one episode, she tells a cheerleader, "I'm going to ask you to smell your armpits. That's the smell of failure, and it's stinking up my office." Since she holds a lot of **ANIMOSITY** (hatred) toward the glee club, she takes particular delight in crafting **ACERBIC** and **ACRID** remarks at the expense of Will Schuster, often **DERIDING** (Word 180) his haircut.

Charles McGrath wrote in the *New York Times* that Gore Vidal, "the novelist, essayist, screenwriter, and all-around man of letters who died in July [2012] at the age of 86...was shown in several clips from a PBS documentary being his usual **ACERBIC**, witty and elegant self: taking America to task for needless wars, a bloated military-industrial complex, and political hypocrisy."

212 | SOLEMN, GRAVE, SOMBER
Not cheerful or smiling; serious; gloomy

June 25, 2009, when the King of Pop died, marked a **SOMBER** day for the entire world. Michael Jackson was regarded by many as the premier entertainer in both singing and dancing. Jackson's **INNOVATIVE** (Word 126) musical technique has influenced artists spanning all modern genres. His death was an especially **GRAVE** event because Jackson was preparing for his final tour, *This Is It*.

213 | INQUISITIVE
Curious; inquiring

In the music video for her song "Friday," Rebecca Black makes a silly **INQUISITIVE** remark that becomes the source of some parody. As she arrives at a crosswalk, she sees her friends driving to school. Her friends **EXHORT** (Word 53) her to hop into the car. Rebecca responds by **INQUIRING**:

Kickin' in the front seat?
Sittin' in the back seat?
Gotta make my mind up,
Which seat can I take?

After her music video was called "the worst video ever" by a comedian with a Twitter following, **INQUISITIVE** YouTube users amassed over 167 million views and 3.1 million "dislikes," helping to create an "overnight sensation."

214 | REFLECTIVE, PENSIVE
Engaged in, involving, or reflecting deep or serious thought, usually marked by sadness or MELANCHOLY

The Thinker, a famous bronze and marble sculpture by August Rodin, depicts a **PENSIVE** man, that is, one captured in deep thought. The pose of *The Thinker*, seated with one fist nestled under his chin, has become very famous. The pose of deep **REFLECTION** has led many to believe that the man is struggling with some form of internal conflict. The original sculpture is located in Paris, but there are dozens of authentic cast replicas all over the world, including 13 in North America.

215 | EQUIVOCAL

AMBIGUOUS (Word 21), open to interpretation, having several equally possible meanings

EQUIVOCATE

To avoid making an explicit statement; to hedge; to use vague or AMBIGUOUS (see KNOW YOUR ROOTS, p. 2) language

The classic movie *The Graduate* has a particularly **EQUIVOCAL** ending. Ben Braddock storms the church to stop Elaine Robinson's wedding but arrives just after the vows are said. Nonetheless, the newlywed Elaine sees Ben and decides to run off with him. Laughing, the couple race out of the church and board a bus. But then their smiles fade, and they become strangely silent. The film's **AMBIGUOUS** ending leaves the audience wondering if they really love each other and what will happen to them in the future.

In election campaigns candidates often appear to be **EQUIVOCATING**, as if fearful of losing votes by coming out too **UNEQUIVOCALLY** on one side or another of an issue.

Alfred Hitchcock **COINED** (Word 296) the term of what is now a commonly used plot device in movies: the MacGuffin. A MacGuffin is a critically important object that drives the story forward, but whose exact nature usually remains **AMBIGUOUS** and undefined. In the film *Citizen Kane*, the meaning of the word "Rosebud" is the MacGuffin. In the movie *Pulp Fiction*, the briefcase is an **EQUIVOCAL** MacGuffin. The briefcase is very important to the characters, yet we never see the contents of the precious luggage. Fans of the movie often hypothesize and debate about the **AMBIGUOUS** contents of the briefcase.

216 | DEFERENTIAL

Respectful; dutiful

That Prince William's wife, Kate Middleton, Duchess of Cambridge and future queen of England, is a former commoner means that she must show proper **DEFERENCE** to the royal family, including Princesses Beatrice and Eugenie, the daughters of Prince Andrew. This **DEFERENTIAL** protocol is outlined in the "Order Of Precedence Of The Royal Family," which was recently revised by Queen Elizabeth to take into account Kate's non-royal origins.

On the hit Masterpiece Theater TV show *Downton Abbey*, the valet Bates must show proper **DEFERENCE** to Lord Grantham, even though the two served together in the Boer war. In the highly **STRATIFIED** (hierarchal, separated into a sequence of social levels) world of early 20th century British society, his role as a servant requires that he be **DEFERENTIAL**.

217 | EBULLIENT, ELATED, ECSTATIC, EUPHORIC, EXUBERANT
Feeling or expressing great happiness or triumph

Tip for a Direct Hit

The word EBULLIENT comes from the Latin verb *ebullire*, to bubble forth or be boisterous, going back to *bullire*, to boil. So an EBULLIENT person is bubbly, upbeat, and high-spirited.

The London Olympic Women's Soccer final was a **EUPHORIC** day for the U.S. team. The Americans won the gold medal against Japan and **AVENGED** (take vengeance or exact satisfaction for) their defeat in the 2011 FIFA Women's World Cup final. The American team was **ELATED** to win the third consecutive Olympic gold medal for the United States.

Even though the Japanese women were **CRESTFALLEN** (sad and disappointed) at the end of the final game; they were **EBULLIENT** as they stood on the medal stand to receive their Olympic silver medals. (They also got to fly home in Business Class). The Canadian women's team was **ECSTATIC** when they received their bronze medals since they were the first Canadian team sport to bring back a medal since the 1936 Berlin Olympic games.

218 | BENEVOLENT
Well-meaning; kindly (see KNOW YOUR ROOTS, p. 61)

MALEVOLENT
Wishing evil to others, showing ill will

Mother Teresa was a **BENEVOLENT** Catholic nun who served the people of India for over 45 years, ministering to the poor, sick, and orphaned, while spreading a message of love. Mother Teresa also founded a program called Missionaries of Charity, which supported soup kitchens, orphanages, schools, and homes for people with HIV/AIDS. Mother Teresa's **BENEVOLENCE** can be noted in such sayings as:

"*Love is a fruit in season at all times, and within reach of every hand.***"**

Perhaps the most **MALEVOLENT** of all historical figures was Hitler, who ordered the deaths of millions of people during the Holocaust.

In Shakespeare's *Othello*, Iago **MALEVOLENTLY** manipulates Othello into believing that his loving and innocent wife, Desdemona, is unfaithful. The question of Iago's motives remains one of the most mysterious of literary enigmas. Perhaps he is simply evil.

219 | WHIMSICAL
Playful; fanciful; CAPRICIOUS (Word 63); given to whimsies or odd notions

In Disney/Pixar's *Up*, Carl Fredricksen lives in a quirky old house painted in lots of bright colors surrounded by modern, sleek skyscrapers. His multicolored cottage adds a touch of **WHIMSY** to the sterility of the neighborhood. His unique house becomes even more **WHIMSICAL** when he ties it to thousands of colorful balloons and flies it through town. The citizens are delighted by the fanciful flying house.

220 | VINDICTIVE
Having a strong desire for revenge

Francis Ford Coppola's *The Godfather* chronicles the rise of Michael Corleone in his family's organized crime business. Michael is initially **AMBIVALENT** (Word 1) about joining the Mafia, but after his father is almost assassinated, he declares his loyalty to the Corleone family business. As he accumulates more power and rises to the top of the family, he becomes increasingly ruthless and **VINDICTIVE**. When he becomes the Don of the Corleone family, he orchestrates a series of hits on all of his enemies in order to "settle all family business." His **VINDICTIVE** and vengeful behavior continues throughout *The Godfather* trilogy, as he takes revenge on everyone with whom he has grievances.

Country-pop star Taylor Swift is known for her autobiographical love songs, but her song "Better Than Revenge" reveals a surprisingly **VINDICTIVE** side. In the song, Taylor describes a cruel girl who stole her boyfriend. In the chorus, Taylor warns, "She should keep in mind there is nothing I do better than revenge." By filling her lyrics with **CAUSTIC** (Word 242) remarks about the girl, Taylor seems to have gotten revenge through this song.

221 | PROSAIC, MUNDANE
Dull; uninteresting; ordinary; commonplace; tedious; PEDESTRIAN (Word 303); VAPID (Word 329); BANAL (Word 36); HACKNEYED (Word 36); unexceptional

Originally **PROSAIC** simply referred to PROSE, writing that was not POETRY. It referred to more factual, unimaginative writing, having the character and form of PROSE. Then it did not have negative **NUANCES** (Word 361), but it has now come to be used almost always in a **PEJORATIVE** (negative, **DISPARAGING** (Word 93) sense.

You might refer to your tedious, unglamorous job as **PROSAIC** or to the **MUNDANE** monotony of your **PROSAIC** life or to the unhelpful, **HACKNEYED** (Word 36) nature of someone's **PROSAIC** advice. If you are an F. Scott Fitzgerald fan, you might want to label Ernest Hemingway's simple, straightforward prose style as **PROSAIC** but Fitzgerald's more lyrical prose style as **POETIC**.

222 | VITRIOLIC

Bitter; CAUSTIC (Word 242); ACERBIC (Word 211); filled with malice

In the movie *Horrible Bosses*, Nick Hendricks suffers as an employee of his incredibly demanding and **VITUPERATIVE** (Word 355) boss, Dave Harken. Dave mocks Nick constantly and berates him with **VITRIOLIC** outbursts. When Nick tries to quit his job in order to escape the abuse, Dave threatens, "Let me tell you something, you stupid little runt. I own you. … So don't walk around here thinking you have free will because you don't. I could crush you anytime I want. So settle in, 'cause you are here for the long haul."

223 | CONCILIATORY

Appeasing; intending to PLACATE (Word 390)

In *Animal House*, Dean Wormer meets with the town's mayor to arrange the annual Faber College homecoming parade. The mayor tells him, "If you want the homecoming parade in my town, you have to pay." At first, Wormer says that it's wrong to extort money from the college, but the mayor continues to demand payment. Wormer eventually assumes a **CONCILIATORY** tone and offers to "arrange a nice honorarium from the student fund." The offer **PLACATES** (Word 390) the mayor, and he agrees to hold the parade in the town.

224 | DESPAIRING
Showing the loss of all hope

After the stock market crash of 1929, the majority of the American public was **DESPAIRING**. One author described the general public emotion as "fear mixed with a **VERTIGINOUS** (Word 402) disorientation." So many had lost their life savings, and were thrust into a life of poverty. The feelings of **DESPAIR** only increased throughout the 12-year-long Great Depression, which concluded with the American mobilization for World War II.

225 | INFLAMMATORY
Arousing; intended to inflame a situation or ignite angry or violent feelings

Are you familiar with the online practice of "trolling"? *PC* magazine defines a troll as an online user who posts **INFLAMMATORY** and **DEROGATORY** (disrespectful) remarks simply to stimulate emotions. For example, a troll might visit a YouTube video regarding the latest Mac release and post an **INFLAMMATORY** remark about Apple computers just to provoke angry responses.

INFLAMMATORY RHETORIC (the art of speaking and writing) has become **PERVASIVE** (widespread) in political debates over such **PARTISAN** (Word 108) issues as abortion, illegal immigration, health-care, and raising or lowering taxes.

FAST REVIEW

Quick Definitions

Volume 1 contains 225 words, each of which is illustrated with vivid pop culture, historic, and literary examples. The Fast Review is designed to provide you with an easy and efficient way to review each of these words. We recommend that you put a check beside each word that you know. That way you can quickly identify the words you are having trouble remembering. Focus on each hard-to-remember word by going over its definition, reviewing its examples, and trying to come up with your own memory tip.

Good luck with your review. Don't expect to learn all of these words at once. Frequent repetition is the best way to learn and remember new words.

CHAPTER 1: CORE VOCABULARY I

1. **AMBIVALENT**—Having mixed or opposing feelings at the same time

2. **ANOMALY**—Deviation from the norm or what is expected
   ANOMALOUS—ATYPICAL, full of ANOMALIES

3. **SARCASTIC, SARDONIC, SNIDE**—Mocking; derisive; taunting; stinging

4. **DEARTH, PAUCITY**—A scarcity or shortage of something

5. **PRATTLE**—To speak in a foolish manner; to babble incessantly

6. **WRY, DROLL**—Dry; humorous with a clever twist and a touch of irony

7. **UNCONVENTIONAL, UNORTHODOX**—Not ordinary or typical;
   characterized by avoiding customary conventions and behaviors

8. **METICULOUS, PAINSTAKING, FASTIDIOUS—**Extremely careful;
   very EXACTING

9. **AUDACIOUS**—Fearlessly, often recklessly daring; very bold

10. **INDIFFERENT, APATHETIC**—Marked by a lack of interest or concern;
    NONCHALANT

11. **DIFFIDENT, SELF-EFFACING**—Hesitant due to a lack of self-confidence;
    unassertive; shy; retiring

12. **PRAGMATIC**—Practical; sensible; NOT idealistic or romantic

13. **EVOCATION**—An imaginative re-creation of something; a calling forth

14. **PRESUMPTUOUS**—Taking liberties; brashly overstepping one's place;
    impertinently bold; displaying EFFRONTERY

15. **RECALCITRANT**—Stubbornly resistance and defiant; OBSTINATE;
    OBDURATE; REFRACTORY; disobedient

16. **BOON**—A timely benefit; blessing
    BANE—A source of harm and ruin

17. **CLANDESTINE, SURREPTITIOUS**—Secret; covert; not open; NOT
    ABOVEBOARD

18. **AFFABLE, AMIABLE, GENIAL, GREGARIOUS**—Agreeable; marked by
    a pleasing personality; warm and friendly

19. **AUSTERE**—Having no adornment or ornamentation; bare;
    not ORNATE
    AUSTERITY—Great self-denial, economy, discipline; lack of adornment

20. **ALTRUISM**—Unselfish concern for the welfare of others

21. **AMBIGUITY**— The quality or state of having more than one

possible meaning; doubtful; EQUIVOCAL
AMBIGUOUS—Unclear; uncertain; open to more than one
interpretation; not definitive; DUBIOUS

22. **UPBRAID, REPROACH, CASTIGATE**—To express disapproval; to scold;
    to rebuke; to CENSURE

23. **NOSTALGIA**— A WISTFUL, sentimental longing for a place or time in
    the past

24. **CONJECTURE**—An inference based upon guesswork; a SUPPOSITION

25. **OBSOLETE, ARCHAIC, ANTIQUATED**—No longer in use; outmoded in
    design or style

26. **AUSPICIOUS, PROPITIOUS**—Very favorable

27. **GAFFE**—A blunder; a *faux pas*; a clumsy social or diplomatic error

28. **IMPASSE**—A deadlock; stalemate; failure to reach an agreement

29. **ANACHRONISM**—The false assignment of an event, person, scene, or
    language to a time when the event, person, scene, or word did not exist

30. **BELIE**—To contradict; to prove false, used of appearances that are
    misrepresentative

31. **MITIGATE, MOLLIFY, ASSUAGE, ALLEVIATE**—To relieve; to lessen; to ease

32. **COVET**—To strongly desire; to crave
    COVETOUS—Grasping, greedy, eager to obtain something; AVARICIOUS

33. **ANTITHESIS**—The direct or exact opposite; extreme contrast; ANTIPODE
    ANTITHETICAL—Exactly opposite; ANTIPODAL

34. **PROTOTYPE**—An original model; an initial design

35. **ALOOF**—Detached; distant physically or emotionally; reserved;
    standing near but apart

36. **TRITE, HACKNEYED, BANAL, PLATITUDINOUS, INSIPID**—Unoriginal;
    commonplace; overused; CLICHÉD

37. **ANTECEDENT**—A preceding event; a FORERUNNER; a PRECURSOR

38. **PLAUSIBLE**—Believable; credible
    IMPLAUSIBLE—Unbelievable; incredible

39. **PRUDENT**—Careful; cautious; sensible

40. **AESTHETIC**—Relating to the nature of beauty, art, and taste; having
    a sense of what is beautiful, attractive, or pleasing

41. **PARADOX**—A seemingly contradictory statement that nonetheless
    expresses a truth

42. **ENIGMATIC, INSCRUTABLE**—Mysterious; puzzling; unfathomable; baffling

43. **ACQUIESCE**—To comply; to agree; to give in

44. **NAÏVE, GULLIBLE**—Unaffectedly simple; lacking worldly expertise; overly CREDULOUS; unsophisticated; immature; inexperienced; INGENUOUS

45. **AUTONOMY**—Independence; self-governance
    AUTONOMOUS—Acting independently, or having the freedom to do so; not controlled by others; self-governing

46. **FUTILE**—Completely useless; doomed to failure; in vain

47. **INDIGENOUS, ENDEMIC**—Native to an area

48. **UBIQUITOUS, PREVALENT**—Characterized by being everywhere; omnipresent; widespread; PERVASIVE

49. **PANDEMIC**—An epidemic that is geographically widespread and affects a large proportion of the population

50. **FORTITUDE**—Strength of mind that allows one to endure pain or adversity with courage

CHAPTER 2: CORE VOCABULARY II

51. **DIMINUTIVE**—Very small

52. **TRIVIAL**—Trifling; unimportant; insignificant
    MINUTIAE—Minor everyday details

53. **EXHORT**—To encourage; to urge; to give a pep talk; to IMPLORE

54. **ANTIPATHY**—Strong dislike; ill will; the state of DETESTING someone; ENMITY; RANCOR

55. **DIGRESS**—To depart from a subject; to wander; to ramble

56. **TENACIOUS**—Characterized by holding fast; showing great determination in holding on to something that is valued

57. **INDULGENT**—Characterized by excessive generosity; overly tolerant

58. **POLARIZE**—To create disunity or dissension; to break up into opposing factions or groups; to be DIVISIVE

59. **NEBULOUS**—Vague; cloudy; misty; lacking a fully-developed form

60. **ANALOGY**—A similarity or likeness between things—events, ideas, actions, trends—that are otherwise unrelated
    ANALOGOUS—Comparable or similar in certain respects

61. **EPHEMERAL, FLEETING, EVANESCENT**—Very brief; lasting for a short time; transient
    PERENNIAL—Returning year after year; enduring

62. **PENCHANT, PREDILECTION, PROPENSITY**—A liking or preference for something; a BENT; an INCLINATION

63. **CAPRICIOUS, MERCURIAL, FICKLE**—Very changeable; characterized by constantly-shifting moods

64. **BOORISH, UNCOUTH, CRASS**—Vulgar; characterized by crude behavior and deplorable manners; unrefined

65. **INDIGNANT**—Characterized by outrage at something that is perceived as unjust

66. **INNUENDO**—A veiled reference; an insinuation

67. **THWART, STYMIE**—To stop; to frustrate; to prevent

68. **ADROIT, DEFT, ADEPT**—To have or show great skill; DEXTEROUS; nimble

69. **ADMONISH**—To earnestly caution; to warn another to avoid a course of action

70. **INCONTROVERTIBLE**—Impossible to deny or disprove; demonstrably true

71. **VORACIOUS, RAVENOUS, RAPACIOUS**—A huge appetite that cannot be satisfied; INSATIABLE

72. **CALLOUS**—Emotionally hardened; insensitive; unfeeling

73. **INTREPID, UNDAUNTED**—Courageous; RESOLUTE; fearless

74. **NONCHALANT**—Having an air of casual indifference; coolly unconcerned; UNFLAPPABLE

75. **CONVOLUTED**—Winding, twisting, and therefore difficult to understand; intricate

76. **ITINERANT**—Migrating from place to place; NOT SEDENTARY

77. **POIGNANT**—Moving; touching; heartrending

78. **IMPETUS**—A stimulus or encouragement that results in increased activity

79. **BUCOLIC, RUSTIC, PASTORAL**—Characteristic of charming, unspoiled countryside and the simple, rural life

80. **EQUANIMITY**—Calmness; composure; even-tempered; poise

81. **PANACHE, VERVE, FLAMBOYANCE, ÉLAN**—Great vigor and energy; dash, especially in artistic performance and composition

82. **PROVOCATIVE**—Provoking discussion; stimulating controversy; arousing a reaction

83. **PLACID, SERENE**—Calm or quiet; undisturbed by tumult or disorder

84. **FORTUITOUS**—Of accidental but fortunate occurrence; having unexpected good fortune

85. **DISPEL**—To drive away; scatter, as to DISPEL a misconception

86. **AMALGAM**—A mixture; a blend; a combination of different elements

87. **VIABLE, FEASIBLE**—Capable of being accomplished; possible

88. **ANGUISH**—Agonizing physical or mental pain; torment

89. **INTEMPERATE**—Lacking restraint; excessive
TEMPERATE—Exercising moderation and restraint

90. **SUPERFICIAL**—Shallow; lacking in depth; concerned with surface appearances

91. **LAUD, EXTOL, TOUT, ACCLAIM**—To praise; to applaud

92. **DISMISSIVE**—Showing overt intentional INDIFFERENCE or disregard; rejecting

93. **DISPARAGE**—To speak of in a slighting or disrespectful way; to belittle

94. **POMPOUS**—Filled with excessive self-importance; PRETENTIOUS; OSTENTATIOUS; boastful

95. **CRYPTIC**—Having a hidden or AMBIGUOUS meaning; mysterious

96. **SUBTLE**—Difficult to detect; faint; mysterious; likely to elude perception

97. **DISPARITY**—An inequality; a gap; an imbalance

98. **CURTAIL**—To cut short or reduce

99. **INNOCUOUS**—Harmless; not likely to give offense or to arouse strong feelings or hostility; not INIMICAL

100. **DIATRIBE, TIRADE, HARANGUE**—A bitter abusive denunciation; a thunderous verbal attack; a RANT

CHAPTER 3: YOU MEET THE MOST INTERESTING PEOPLE ON THE SAT

101. **CHARLATAN**—A fake; fraud; imposter; cheat

102. **SKEPTIC**—A person who doubts, asks questions, and lacks faith

103. **RHETORICIAN**—An eloquent writer or speaker; a master of RHETORIC (the art of speaking and writing)

104. **HEDONIST**—A person who believes that pleasure is the chief goal of life
105. **ASCETIC**—A person who gives up material comforts and leads a life of self-denial, especially as an act of religious devotion
106. **RACONTEUR**—A person who excels in telling ANECDOTES
107. **ICONOCLAST**—A person who attacks and ridicules cherished figures, ideas, and institutions
108. **PARTISAN**—A supporter of a person, party, or cause; a person with strong and perhaps biased beliefs
109. **POLYMATH**—A person whose expertise spans a significant number of subject areas
     DILETTANTE—An amateur or dabbler; a person with a SUPERFICIAL interest in an art or a branch of knowledge; a trifler
110. **MENTOR**—An advisor; a teacher; a guide
     ACOLYTE—A devoted follower
111. **DEMAGOGUE**—A leader who appeals to the fears, emotions, and prejudices of the populace
112. **AUTOMATON**—A self-operating machine; a mindless follower; a person who acts in a mechanical fashion
113. **RECLUSE**—A person who leads a secluded or solitary life
114. **BUNGLER**—Someone who is clumsy or INEPT; a person who makes mistakes because of incompetence
115. **CLAIRVOYANT**—Having the supposed power to see objects and events that cannot be perceived with the five traditional senses; as a noun, a SEER
116. **PROGNOSTICATOR**—A person who makes predictions based upon current information and data
117. **PUNDIT**—An expert commentator; an authority who expresses his or her opinion, usually on political issues
118. **ZEALOT**—A very enthusiastic person; a champion; a true believer, perhaps to an excessive degree; a fanatic
119. **NEOPHYTE, NOVICE, GREENHORN**—A beginner; someone new to a field or activity
120. **BENEFACTOR, PATRON**—A person who makes a gift or bequest
     BENEFICIARY—The recipient of funds, titles, property, and other benefits
121. **DISSEMBLER, PREVARICATOR**—A liar and deceiver

122. **PROPONENT**—One who argues in support of something; an ADVOCATE; a champion of a cause

123. **PRODIGY**—A person with great talent; a young genius

124. **ORACLE**—A person considered to be ORACULAR, a source of wise counsel or prophetic opinions

125. **MISANTHROPE**—A person who hates or distrusts humankind

126. **INNOVATOR**—A person who introduces something new

127. **SYCOPHANT**—A person who seeks favor by flattering people of influence; a TOADY; someone who behaves in an OBSEQUIOUS or SERVILE manner

128. **STOIC, STOLID**—Seemingly INDIFFERENT to or unaffected by joy, grief, pleasure, or pain; mpassive and emotionless

129. **REPROBATE**—A morally unprincipled person

130. **RENEGADE**—A disloyal person who betrays his or her cause; a traitor; a deserter

CHAPTER 4: EVERY SAT WORD HAS A HISTORY

131. **DRACONIAN**—Characterized by very strict laws, rules, and punishments

132. **LACONIC**—Very brief; concise; SUCCINCT; TERSE

133. **SPARTAN**—Plain; simple; AUSTERE

134. **HALCYON**—Idyllically calm and peaceful; an untroubled golden time of satisfaction, happiness, and tranquility

135. **SOPHISTRY**—A plausible but deliberately misleading or FALLACIOUS argument designed to deceive someone

136. **CHIMERICAL**—Given to fantastic schemes; existing only in the imagination; impossible; vainly conceived

137. **OSTRACIZE**—To deliberately exclude from a group; to BANISH

138. **IMPECUNIOUS**—Poor; penniless; NOT AFFLUENT

139. **NEFARIOUS**—Famous for being wicked; VILLAINOUS; vile

140. **JOVIAL**—Good-humored; cheerful; JOCULAR

141. **DIRGE**—A funeral hymn; a slow, mournful, LUGUBRIOUS musical composition

142. **MAUDLIN**—Tearful; excessively sentimental, but not MAWKISH

143. **QUIXOTIC**—Foolishly impractical in the pursuit of ideals; impractical idealism

144. **PANDEMONIUM**—A wild uproar; tumult

145. **MARTINET**—A strict disciplinarian; a person who demands absolute adherence to forms and rules

146. **FIASCO**—A complete failure; a DEBACLE

147. **BOWDLERIZE**—To remove or delete parts of a book, song or other work that are considered offensive; to EXPURGATE

148. **GALVANIZE**—To electrify; to stir into action as if with an electric shock

149. **PICAYUNE**—Small value or importance; petty; trifling

150. **GERRYMANDER**—To divide a geographic area into voting districts so as to give unfair advantage to one party in elections

151. **MAVERICK**—An independent individual who does not go along with a group or party; a nonconformist

152. **JUGGERNAUT**—An irresistible force that crushes everything in its path

153. **SERENDIPITY**—Discovery by fortunate accident

154. **ZENITH**—The highest point; the peak; the APEX

155. **NADIR**—The lowest point; the bottom

CHAPTER 5: THE MIGHTY LITTLE AFFIXES

156. **EXPUNGE, EXCISE, EXPURGATE**—To take OUT; to delete; to remove

157. **ECCENTRIC**—Literally OUT of the center; departing from a recognized, conventional, or established norm; an odd, UNCONVENTIONAL person

158. **EXTRICATE**—To get OUT of a difficult situation or entanglement

159. **EXEMPLARY**—Standing OUT from the norm; outstanding; worthy of imitation

160. **ENUMERATE**—To count OUT; to list; to tick off the reasons for

161. **ELUSIVE**—OUT of reach and therefore difficult to catch, define, or describe

162. **EXORBITANT**—Literally OUT of orbit and therefore unreasonably expensive

163. **REDUNDANT**—Needlessly repetitive; saying things AGAIN and AGAIN

164. **REPUDIATE, RECANT, RENOUNCE**—To take BACK; to reject; to DISAVOW

165. **RELINQUISH**—To surrender or give BACK (or return) a possession, right, or privilege

166. **RESILIENT**—Bouncing BACK from ADVERSITY or misfortune; recovering quickly

167. **REAFFIRM**—To assert AGAIN; to confirm; to state positively

168. **RETICENT**—To hold BACK one's thoughts, feelings and personal affairs; restrained or reserved

169. **REBUFF**—To repel or drive BACK; to bluntly reject

170. **RENOVATE**—To make new AGAIN; restore by repairing and remodeling

171. **REJUVENATE**—To make young AGAIN; to restore youthful vigor and appearance

172. **RESURGENT**—Rising AGAIN; sweeping or surging BACK

173. **REPUGNANT**—ABHORRENT; offensive to the mind or senses; causing distaste or AVERSION

174. **DELETERIOUS**—Going DOWN in the sense of having a harmful effect; injurious

175. **DECRY**—To put DOWN in the sense of openly condemning; to express strong disapproval

176. **DESPONDENT, MOROSE**—DOWNCAST; very dejected; FORLORN

177. **DENOUNCE**—To put DOWN in the sense of a making a formal accusation; to speak against

178. **DEMISE**—Sent DOWN in the sense of ending in death; the cessation of existence or activity

179. **DEBUNK**—To put DOWN by exposing false and exaggerated claims

180. **DERIDE, DERISIVE**—To put DOWN with contemptuous jeering; to ridicule or laugh at

181. **DEVOID**—DOWN in the sense of being empty; completely lacking in substance or quality; BEREFT; vacant

182. **IMPECCABLE**—Having NO flaws; perfect

183. **IMPLACABLE**—NOT capable of being PLACATED or appeased

184. **INEXORABLE**—NOT capable of being stopped; relentless; inevitable

185. **INCOHERENT**—NOT coherent and therefore lacking organization; lacking logical or meaningful connections

186. **INSURMOUNTABLE**—NOT capable of being surmounted or overcome

187. **IRREVERENT**—Lacking proper respect or seriousness; disrespectful

188. **IRRESOLUTE**—NOT RESOLUTE; uncertain how to act or proceed; INDECISIVE; VACILLATING

189. **CIRCUMSPECT**—Looking carefully AROUND—thus cautious and careful; PRUDENT; discreet

190. **CIRCUITOUS**—CIRCULAR and therefore indirect in language, behavior, or action, roundabout

191. **CIRCUMVENT**—To circle AROUND and therefore bypass; to avoid by artful maneuvering

192. **CIRCUMSCRIBE**—To draw a line AROUND and therefore to narrowly limit or restrict actions

193. **MAGNANIMOUS**—FILLED WITH generosity and forgiveness; forgoing resentment and revenge

194. **ERRONEOUS**—FILLED WITH errors; wrong

195. **MOMENTOUS**—FILLED WITH importance; very significant

196. **MELLIFLUOUS**—Smooth and sweet; flowing like honey

197. **OMINOUS**—FILLED WITH menace; threatening

198. **ACRIMONIOUS**—FILLED WITH bitterness; sharpness in words; RANCOROUS

199. **COPIOUS**—FILLED WITH abundance; plentiful

200. **ABSTEMIOUS**—FILLED WITH moderation; TEMPERATE in eating and drinking

201. **MALODOROUS**—FILLED WITH an unpleasant odor; foul-smelling

202. **TEDIOUS**—FILLED WITH boredom; very tiresome; dull and fatiguing

203. **HEINOUS, EGREGIOUS**—Flagrantly, conspicuously bad; abominable; shockingly evil; monstrous; outrageous

204. **GRATUITOUS**—Unwarranted; not called for by the circumstances; unnecessary

205. **PRECARIOUS, PERILOUS**—Uncertain; characterized by a lack of security or stability

CHAPTER 6: THE TONE WORDS

206. **WISTFUL**—Longing and yearning, tinged with MELANCHOLY (long-lasting sadness) and PENSIVENESS

207. **EARNEST**—Serious in intention or purpose; showing depth and SINCERITY of feelings

208. **DISGRUNTLED, DISCONTENTED**—Angry; dissatisfied; annoyed; impatien; irritated

209. **AUTHORITATIVE**—Commanding and self-confident; likely to be respected and obeyed, based on competent authority

210. **FRIVOLITY**—The trait of being FRIVOLOUS; not serious or sensible
     FRIVOLOUS—Lacking any serious purpose or value; given to trifling or levity
211. **ACERBIC, ACRID**—Harsh; bitter; sharp; CAUSTIC
212. **SOLEMN, GRAVE, SOMBER**—Not cheerful or smiling; serious; gloomy
213. **INQUISITIVE**—Curious; inquiring
214. **REFLECTIVE, PENSIVE**—Engaged in, involving, or reflecting deep or serious thought, usually marked by sadness or MELANCHOLY
215. **EQUIVOCAL**—AMBIGUOUS; open to interpretation; having an uncertain significance or meaning
     EQUIVOCATE—To avoid making an explicit statement; to hedge; to use vague or AMBIGUOUS language
216. **DEFERENTIAL**—Respectful; dutiful
217. **EBULLIENT, ELATED, ECSTATIC, EUPHORIC, EXUBERANT**—Feeling or expressing great happiness or triumph
218. **BENEVOLENT**—Well-meaning; kindly
     MALEVOLENT—Wishing evil to others, showing ill will
219. **WHIMSICAL**—Playful; fanciful; CAPRICIOUS; given to whimsies or odd notions
220. **VINDICTIVE**—Having a strong desire for revenge
221. **PROSAIC, MUNDANE**—Dull; uninteresting; ordinary; commonplace; tedious; PEDESTRIAN; VAPID; BANAL; HACKNEYED; unexceptional
222. **VITRIOLIC**—Bitter; CAUSTIC; ACERBIC; filled with malice
223. **CONCILIATORY**—Appeasing; intending to PLACATE
224. **DESPAIRING**—Showing the loss of all hope
225. **INFLAMMATORY**—Arousing; intended to inflame a situation or ignite angry or violent feelings

TESTING YOUR VOCABULARY

Each SAT contains 19 sentence completion questions that are primarily a test of your vocabulary. Each sentence completion will always have a key word or phrase that will lead you to the correct answer The following 30 sentence completion questions are designed to give you practice using your knowledge of the core vocabulary in Volume 1. Each sentence completion will have a key word or phrase that will lead you to the correct answer. Make sure to circle your answer. You'll find answers and explanations on pages 142–145.

1. Paradoxically, this successful politician is sometimes very sociable and other times very _____.

    A aloof

    B genial

    C trite

    D pragmatic

    E naïve

2. Uncertainty is an unavoidable part of the stock market; investors should, therefore, learn to accept doubt and tolerate _____.

    A futility

    B pragmatism

    C diffidence

    D ambiguity

    E sarcasm

3. Paleontologists like China's Xu Xing now find themselves in the _____ situation of using state-of-the art equipment to analyze prehistoric fossils.

    A futile

    B nostalgic

    C coveted

    D paradoxical

    E banal

4. General MacArthur's bold disregard for popular conventions and time-honored military strategies earned him a reputation for _____.

    A acquiescence

    B audacity

    C prudence

    D indifference

    E ambivalence

5. The scientist was both _____ and _____ : she was always careful to test each hypothesis and cautious not to jump to conclusions.

    A painstaking .. despondent

    B nostalgic .. sentimental

    C clandestine .. unconventional

    D recalcitrant .. presumptuous

    E meticulous .. prudent

6. Serena Williams is often described as having _____ that is apparent in both her dazzling tennis performances and her flamboyant athletic-wear designs.

    A an equanimity

    B a panache

    C a superficiality

    D a nonchalance

    E a subtlety

7. The Post-Modern architectural style is _____ : it combines diverse elements, including classical columns, Baroque ornamentation, and Palladian windows.

   A a diatribe

   B a conjecture

   C an impasse

   D an anachronism

   E an amalgam

8. Boisterous, uncouth, and devoid of all manners, Artem was widely known for his _____ behavior.

   A boorish

   B intrepid

   C subtle

   D temperate

   E laudable

9. The coach's halftime speech to his team was a _____ , a bitter railing denouncing their inept play.

   A diatribe

   B conjecture

   C innuendo

   D evocation

   E antecedent

10. Hira's supervisor faulted her for turning in a _____ proposal that was overly vague and lacked a detailed analysis of costs and benefits.

    A morose

    B pompous

    C nebulous

    D viable

    E divisive

11. The new zoning ordinance provoked such intense debate and caused such partisanship that it was branded the most _____ in the community's long history.

    A innocuous

    B subtle

    C superficial

    D archaic

    E polarizing

12. Emily was renowned for her _____ ; she remained calm and composed even when confronted with stressful personal problems.

    A callousness

    B capriciousness

    C intemperance

    D equanimity

    E superficiality

13. Like a true _____ , Drew had a number of constantly shifting interests and hobbies.

  A dilettante

  B hedonist

  C ascetic

  D philanthropist

  E dissembler

14. Critics accused the used car salesman of being a _____ because he tried to dupe customers with fraudulent information.

  A novice

  B charlatan

  C prodigy

  D sycophant

  E clairvoyant

15. Much of Frederick Douglass' prestige and influence came from his skill with the spoken word; he was a great _____ at a time when eloquent oratory was widely _____ .

  A raconteur .. disparaged

  B pundit .. spurned

  C rhetorician .. valued

  D mediator .. ignored

  E prognosticator .. denounced

16. The _____ prediction was astonishingly _____ : it offered a bold view of the future that no one had foreseen.

  A prognosticator's .. unconventional

  B partisan's .. obvious

  C iconoclast's .. orthodox

  D pundit's .. fleeting

  E demagogue's .. prudent

17. As _____ , Ashley delighted in disputing sacrosanct beliefs, questioning established authorities, and challenging long-held practices.

  A a mediator

  B a sycophant

  C a mentor

  D an iconoclast

  E a beneficiary

18. The head coach responded to the breach of team rules by instituting unusually strict rules that players felt were too _____ .

  A cryptic

  B diminutive

  C draconian

  D jocular

  E equivocal

19. Outraged editors charged the vice-principal with _____ their work by deleting key parts of a controversial article on teenage drinking.

A coveting

B lauding

C bowdlerizing

D ostracizing

E gerrymandering

20. Morgan was _____ person, naturally inclined to be tearful and excessively sentimental.

A a quixotic

B a recalcitrant

C an acerbic

D a deft

E a maudlin

21. Some people alternate between contrasting temperaments; either they are _____ or they are _____ .

A nefarious .. wicked

B morose .. despondent

C affable .. genial

D quixotic .. pragmatic

E jovial .. jocular

22. Sydney is best described as _____ : she is an independent person who recognizes that the majority is sometimes wrong.

A a martinet

B a maverick

C a stoic

D a charlatan

E an ascetic

23. Charlie looked back on his family's vacation at the lake as _____ time filled with carefree days and untroubled tranquility.

A a halcyon

B an anguished

C a divisive

D an intemperate

E an ambiguous

24. Scientists warn that the _____ consequences of global warming will not be limited to the deterioration of penguin and polar bear habitats; humans can also expect devastating hurricanes and _____ floods.

A fortuitous .. damaging

B fleeting .. prodigious

C painstaking .. beneficial

D incontrovertible .. innocuous

E deleterious .. destructive

25. Muckrakers like Upton Sinclair and Ida Tarbell _____ the corrupt business practices of early 20th century robber barons, _____ their unbridled greed and indifferent attitude toward the public good.

A disapproved .. lauding

B extolled .. disparaging

C reaffirmed .. deriding

D celebrated .. censuring

E decried .. denouncing

26. Cautious, conventional, and always careful to follow procedures, Matthew is the very model of _____ government bureaucrat.

A an audacious

B a resilient

C a circumspect

D a sardonic

E an acrimonious

27. What is the most inspiring about Professor DeMarco's portrayal of Venetian life is the _____ of the human spirit, the force that has sustained the island-city through adversity and always remains undaunted.

A divisiveness

B resilience

C superficiality

D reticence

E callousness

28. Jessica's report was criticized for being both _____ and _____: it was poorly organized and overly vague.

    A meticulous .. ambiguous

    B circuitous .. adroit

    C incoherent .. nebulous

    D glib .. poignant

    E inexorable .. dismissive

29. Gustave Courbet's bitter and spiteful denunciations of his critics earned him a reputation for being _____.

    A magnanimous

    B abstemious

    C meticulous

    D vitriolic

    E erroneous

30. The Mayans' sudden and irrevocable _____ is a long-standing historic _____: over the years, scholars have suggested a number of possible causes, including excessive warfare and devastating natural disasters, to explain the disappearance of Mayan civilization.

    A demise .. mystery

    B longevity .. enigma

    C rebirth .. riddle

    D collapse .. myth

    E resurgence .. conjecture

ANSWERS AND EXPLANATIONS

1. A

The question asks you to find a word that is the opposite of sociable. The correct answer is ALOOF (Word 35).

2. D

The question asks you to find a word that means uncertain and fits with the phrase "accept doubt." The correct answer is AMBIGUITY (Word 21).

3. D

The question asks you to find a word that satisfies the contradictory but true situation in which Xu Xing uses state-of-the art equipment to analyze prehistoric fossils. The correct answer is PARADOXICAL (Word 41).

4. B

The question asks you to find a word that means a bold disregard for popular conventions and time-honored military strategies. The correct answer is AUDACITY (Word 9).

5. E

The question asks you to find a first word that means careful and a second word that means cautious. Note that in choice A, painstaking does mean careful, but despondent means very depressed. The correct answers are METICULOUS (Word 8) and PRUDENT (Word 39).

6. B

The question asks you to find a word that means "dazzling" and "flamboyant." The correct answer is PANACHE (Word 81).

7. E

The question asks you to find a word that means "combines diverse elements." The correct answer is AMALGAM (Word 86).

8. A

The question asks you to find a word that means "boisterous, uncouth, and devoid of all manners." The correct answer is BOORISH (Word 64).

9. A

The question asks you to find a word that means a bitter denunciation. The correct answer is DIATRIBE (Word 100).

10. C

The question asks you to find a word that means vague and lacking a detailed analysis. The correct answer is NEBULOUS (Word 59).

11. E

The question asks you to find a word that would cause an "intense debate" and spark "partisanship." The correct answer is POLARIZING (Word 58).

12. D

The question asks you to find a word that means to be calm and composed under stressful conditions. The correct answer is EQUANIMITY (Word 80).

13. A

The question asks you to find a word describing a person who has "constantly shifting interests and hobbies." The correct answer is DILETTANTE (Word 109) because a DILETTANTE is a dabbler who has shifting interests.

14. B

The question asks you to find a word describing a person who "tried to dupe customers with fraudulent information." The correct answer is CHARLATAN (Word 101) because a CHARLATAN is a fake or fraud who tries to dupe and cheat unsuspecting people.

15. C

The question asks you to find a first word describing Frederick Douglass. You are told that he was an "eloquent" orator who had great "skill with the spoken word." The second word must be positive because Douglass derived great "prestige and influence" from his oratory. The correct answer is RHETORICIAN (Word 103) and VALUED, because a RHETORICIAN is an eloquent speaker and VALUED is a positive second word. Note that answer A is tempting because a RACONTEUR is a great storyteller. However, DISPARAGED (Word 93) is a negative word meaning to belittle or slight.

16. A

The question asks you to find a first word describing a person who makes predictions and a second word describing those predictions as both "bold" and so farsighted that they had not been "foreseen." The correct answer is PROGNOSTICATOR (Word 116) and UNCONVENTIONAL (Word 7) because a PROGNOSTICATOR makes predictions and these predictions would be UNCONVENTIONAL because they are both "bold" and unforeseen.

17. D

The question asks you to find a person who delights in "disputing sacrosanct beliefs, questioning established authorities, and challenging long-held practices." The correct answer is ICONOCLAST (Word 107) because an ICONOCLAST attacks cherished ideas and institutions.

18. C

The question asks you to find a word that describes the "strict rules" instituted by the head coach. The correct answer is DRACONIAN (Word 131).

19. C

The question asks you to find a word that means "deleting key parts." The correct answer is BOWDLERIZING (Word 147).

20. E

The question asks you to find a word that means to be "naturally inclined to be tearful and excessively sentimental." The correct answer is MAUDLIN (Word 142).

21. D

The question asks you to find a pair of antonyms describing "contrasting temperaments." Choices A, B, C and E are all pairs of synonyms. Only choice D provides a pair of antonyms. The correct answer is therefore QUIXOTIC (Word 143) and PRAGMATIC (Word 12).

22. B

The question asks you to find a word describing "an independent person" who doesn't always follow the majority. The correct answer is MAVERICK (Word 151).

23. A

The question asks you to find a word that is consistent with "carefree days and untroubled tranquility." The correct answer is HALCYON (Word 134).

24. E

The question asks you to find a pair of negative words that are consistent with the key words "deterioration" and "devastating." The correct answer is DELETERIOUS (Word 174) and DESTRUCTIVE. Note that DESTRUCTIVE is consistent with "devastating" and that the consequences of global warming are DELETERIOUS for both animals and humans.

25. E

The question asks you to find a pair of words describing how muckrakers would respond to robber barons, who are described as "corrupt," greedy, and "indifferent to the public good." Choices A, B, C, and D all include both positive and negative words. Since the sentence calls for a logically consistent pair of negative words, the correct answer is DECRIED (Word 175) and DENOUNCING (Word 177).

26. C

The question asks you to find a word that describes a bureaucrat who is "cautious, conventional, and always careful to follow procedures." The correct answer is CIRCUMSPECT (Word 189).

27. B

The question asks you to find a word that best describes the spirit of the Venetians. You are told that this spirit or force sustained the Venetians through "adversity and always remains undaunted." The correct answer is RESILIENCE (Word 166).

28. C

The question asks you to find a first word that means "poorly organized" and a second word that means "overly vague." The correct answer is INCOHERENT (Word 185) and NEBULOUS (Word 59).

29. D

The question asks you to find a negative word that best characterizes how Courbet's "bitter and spiteful denunciations" affected his reputation. The correct answer is ACRIMONIOUS (Word 198).

30. A

The question asks you to find a pair of words that are consistent with the Mayans' "disappearance" and the fact that scholars still cannot explain why they vanished. The correct answer is DEMISE (Word 178) and MYSTERY.

INDEX

WORD *Main Page*, *Other Page(s)*